FRANKLIN PIERCE

Franklin Pierce

FRANKLIN PIERCE

The Fourteenth President of the United States

EDWIN P. HOYT

Illustrated with photographs

————ABELARD-SCHUMAN————

London   New York

An INTEXT Publisher

7886

BOOKS BY EDWIN P. HOYT

THE AMERICAN ATTITUDE
The Story of the Making of Foreign Policy in the United States
FRANKLIN PIERCE
The Fourteenth President of the United States
JOHN TYLER
The Tenth President of the United States
LELAND STANFORD
THE TRAGIC COMMODORE
The Story of Oliver Hazard Perry

Second Impression, 1973

© Copyright 1972 by Edwin P. Hoyt
Library of Congress Catalogue Card Number: 74–156582
ISBN: 0 200 71828 2

Published on the same day in Canada by Longman Canada Limited.

NEW YORK
Abelard-Schuman
Limited
257 Park Avenue So.
10010

LONDON
Abelard-Schuman
Limited
450 Edgware Road W2 1EG
and
24 Market Square Aylesbury

Printed in the United States of America

CONTENTS

LIST
OF
ILLUSTRATIONS

1

A BOY
AND
HIS FATHER

In 1634, when religious oppression in England had grown severe, and the migration of Pilgrims across the Atlantic increased considerably, a young man named Thomas Pierce came by ship to Massachusetts and settled in Charlestown, today a part of Boston. He was the first American ancestor of Franklin Pierce, who would become the 14th President of the United States, and who would serve his country to the best of his ability, to be rewarded only by the silent contempt of his countrymen and almost constant unhappiness in the last years of his life.

Franklin Pierce's story is a political and personal tragedy that is unmatched in American life. Politically speaking, the closest resemblance is in the life of Herbert Hoover, who sank into political oblivion after his single term in office. But Hoover's life story was relieved by a final recognition in his later years. No such justice came to relieve the tortures of a sick and unhappy Franklin Pierce, a man scorned by the public.

Poor Franklin Pierce! He was caught in the middle of problems he did not understand; but in all probability there was not a man in America who could have coped with those problems any better than he did. The 14th President was so unlucky as to hold this high office at a time when the issues of slavery and states' rights were tearing the United States apart. Three men served in the presidency in the decade just preceding the Civil War, and any of the three might have made distinguished names for themselves in other times, under different conditions. Millard Fillmore, Franklin Pierce and James Buchanan were all rejected by their fellow countrymen in later years because they failed to stop the inexorable march of events. Usually, historians who say that great days make great men prove their point by telling of the heroic days of Lincoln, for example. The same is true when the threads of history pull men along and determine their standing. There can be no better indication of a more negative trend than in the story of Franklin Pierce. His experience was a real American tragedy.

Franklin was the seventh in the American line started by old Thomas Pierce. The Pierces had stayed in New England, making an indifferent living from the land. Thomas Pierce's grandson Stephen had moved from Charlestown to what is now Lowell. Benjamin Pierce, Franklin's grandfather, had moved to Chelmsford, where he died in 1763, leaving ten children and a widow to take care of them. As was the fashion of the day, the children were sent to relatives, who took the responsibility for bringing them up until they were able to face the world by themselves.

In the case of Franklin's father, that moment came on April 19, 1775, when he was 18 years old. Benjamin was plowing a field on his uncle's farm when a horseman came galloping by and stopped long enough to deliver some news.

The message he shouted to the boy was that the British were coming. They had marched out of Boston to capture the arms the colonists had been hiding in the villages around the city. They had come to Lexington and had fired on the people, killing eight men.

Having delivered his news, the man spurred his horse and was gone, leaving Benjamin Pierce to ponder. The boy did not wait long. He unwrapped the reins of the plow and unyoked the oxen. He took his uncle's fowling piece—an old-fashioned shotgun—picked up the bullet pouch and powder horn that went with it, and marched off to war, determined to avenge his dead countrymen.

Benjamin Pierce did not reach Concord in time to find the British, but the next day he enlisted in the company of Captain John Ford. For eight months, he trained and fought with other rawboned youths. He was at Breed's Hill and tasted the defeat of that battle with the rest of the Americans. He was at Dorchester Heights when the British evacuated Boston, and he marched in triumphantly with the other Americans. He was at Ticonderoga. He defended Fort Stanwix in New York against the Tories and the Indians, in the regiment of Colonel John Brooks. By this time, the young man was a sergeant and a valiant soldier. He was with General Benedict Arnold on Bewis Heights, when the Americans kept watch on Burgoyne's red-coats down below. In the winter of 1777, Benjamin Pierce shivered at Valley Forge; he went to White Plains and then to defend West Point. In 1780, he was made a lieutenant; and when the war ended, he was one of the few officers retained by General George Washington until the end, after New York City had been occupied. Few men enjoyed a more distinguished career in the Revolutionary army than Benjamin Pierce. The experience was to color his life and the life of his son Franklin, who regarded a military affiliation as a necessity in public life.

Mustered out of the army and paid in almost worthless Continental currency, Benjamin Pierce went back to Massachusetts to look for work. He was sent out to explore lands in wild New Hampshire by an absentee owner named Stoddard. In the course of his travels in the green hills, he came upon a little farm of 50 acres whose looks he liked, and he asked the

Benjamin Pierce, father of Franklin Pierce

owner if he would sell. Since the land consisted of a hilly meadow and uncut timber, the poor farmer was eager enough to get a little cash and try again. Benjamin Pierce bought a log cabin in the wilderness in order to begin a private life. He came back the following year and settled down to cut timber and clear land.

The land would scarcely have supported him, but he secured an appointment as a brigade major for the militia of Hillsboro County, and the small salary that the post paid made the difference between success and failure on the farm. A few years later, the townsmen had dignified the name of the county to Hillsborough and, in 1789, as one of the best-known citizens, Colonel—and later General—Benjamin Pierce was elected to the county council. He became sheriff, held other local offices and managed to support himself on the farm.

In 1787, Benjamin Pierce had married Elizabeth Andrews, daughter of one of the settlers of Hillsborough. She died in childbirth, leaving a daughter named Elizabeth. Two years later, Pierce remarried. This time he married Anna Kendrick, the daughter of a local businessman and farmer. They had eight children: Benjamin, Nancy, John Sullivan, Harriet, Charles Grandison, Franklin, Charlotte and Henry Dearborn, in that order. Franklin, who would rise to the presidency, was born November 23, 1804, a year before his father received the great honor of being appointed brigadier general of the New Hampshire militia.

Part of the reason for the appointment was the fact that, for the first time that year, New Hampshire had a Democratic-Republican for governor. Since the political coloration of the times was to have an immense influence on all of Franklin Pierce's career, it is worth explaining the complex politics of the post-Revolutionary period.

George Washington was the first President of the United States, and in his earliest day there was no political partisanship, unless one were to consider the Revolutionary versus Tory relationships. Most Americans considered the Tories to be outright traitors and, therefore, outside the political fold. Benjamin Franklin, for example, was a Revolutionary and his son, who was royal governor of New Jersey, was a Tory. While Ben Franklin is much honored in America today, his son was almost unknown until the Republic approached its two-hundred-year mark, when even the Tories were beginning to be looked upon with a more tolerant eye.

In the beginning, the Revolutionaries argued as individuals. But as they were forced to band together and form a common government, they found it expedient to establish political associations. The first of these of any importance was the Federalist party of George Washington. He, Alexander Hamilton, John Adams and many other leaders believed in a strong federal government. Indeed, Washington once ordered a march on the backwoodsmen of Pennsylvania for defying the federal government, and civil war was averted only by the collapse of the backwoods rebellion.

But among the statesmen of America, there were those who believed in a strong states' rights movement and less federal authority. Chief among these was Thomas Jefferson, and it was Jefferson and the Democratic-Republicans to whom Benjamin Pierce firmly hooked his own political future. Here is old Ben's account of the political break and the reasons for it. In its simplicity it tells very well why he felt the way he did:

I remained in the army during the war. I enjoyed it much. I had the blessing of fine health, returned home full of joyful feelings that we had driven the enemy into their wooden walls and left the soil of our country for peaceful enjoyment of a most happy and free government during the first eight years under General Washington. Mr. Adams followed, and about this time too many of the old Tories [by their false profession] had got into Congress and by their sophistry and deceit had so much power that they passed just such laws as we had fought against. These laws being published, the Republicans began to complain and said, "These are like the laws we have been fighting against."

Upon this the Tories said, "We will let you know about that." And to be sure to preserve their laws they raised a standing army and placed it in the heart of the country to give aid to the support of these laws.

The Tories then with all their followers mounted the Black Cockade [in their hats] in imitation of their friends the British and then called all that would not join their ranks "plough joggers" and "poor spruce shingle folks not worthy of the character of men."

But, thank kind Providence, the Republicans took the hint and did their duty at the ballot box and laid their standing army and tyrannical laws prostrate by the election of Thomas Jefferson.

These fierce sentiments were to guide Benjamin Pierce all his life, and his son was to grow up on them. The old general refused to accept any honors or any favors from Federalists. Thus, his career waxed and waned with the politics of New Hampshire, and Franklin was as much aware of political differences as any youth in the country because he lived with them every day. To him the Federalists were just like the British.

Franklin did not grow up a "log cabin boy" although, like many early Presidents, he was born in the log cabin in the old homestead. But shortly afterward, the general's position improved and the family moved to a frame house in Hillsborough Lower Village. This was the back country of New Hampshire, but it was a settlement, not an isolated farm. The general's house was on the highway, and he entertained friends and

The childhood residence of Franklin Pierce, Hillsborough, New Hampshire
photo: The Granger Collection

acquaintances. Indeed, he ran a kind of tavern part of the time, and travelers, in coaches from Keene and Dunstable, stopped off for refreshments and sometimes remained overnight. Thus Franklin, from an early age, was exposed to a constant stream of news from the outside world and was aware, as most youngsters of the countryside were not, of a nation growing all around him.

Hillsborough was six hours by horse from Concord, the state capital, and a spot where humanity dwelt in relative harmony with nature. Young Franklin learned to fish and hunt and handle a gun at an early age. He began, also, to learn to handle the tools of society: reading, writing and arithmetic. The old general's education had been extremely limited—a few seasons of backwoods schooling, none lasting more than a few weeks. He wrote in a script that was difficult to read, and his grammar and punctuation would have shamed a modern third-grader. He was determined that those of his children who showed an aptitude for learning would have the best education he could give them. Fortunately for Franklin's later career, he was one of the two who took to "learning." Combined with this, however, was an almost reverent feeling for military life, which his father and the general's friends encouraged with their daring tales of the Revolutionary War. Franklin, or young Frank as he was known, looked forward in his early days to becoming a soldier and commanding battalions.

The military life thrilled him; and when Franklin Pierce was eight years old, the war hawks of Washington again brought the nation into another war with Great Britain. In New England, the war was generally unpopular among those who traded or manufactured for a living. This gave the backwoodsmen of New Hampshire, to whom British trade meant nothing, more reason to be contemptuous of the "pale and shamed" Federalists, who opposed the war strenuously and made a campaign issue out of it in the state elections. The general was aghast when John T. Gilman, a Federalist, was elected governor in 1813. In line with the politics of New Hampshire in those days, the new governor set out to ruin all his political enemies, and high up on the list was the Sheriff of Hillsborough County, General Pierce. Governor Gilman controlled the legislature, so he had charges brought against General Pierce and removed him from office. The disgrace was hard to bear—even harder when, in 1814, Gilman was again elected—but then a spot of hope appeared. That same year, General Pierce was selected by New Hampshiremen to be a member of the governor's advisory council, and the governor had to sit at the table with the man whom he had tried to ruin. General Pierce had his chance to embarrass his political enemy and he did so at every opportunity.

Young Franklin was much more interested in the war than in its political implications. The soldiers of New Hampshire moved back and forth along the turnpike that ran before the family's big, white house. And, although his father was often gone to Concord on state business, the women of the family ran the tavern and entertained a stream of soldiers who stopped on their way to Portsmouth, where they guarded against the invasion of the hated Redcoats. The war was brought home, too, when his brother Benjamin, who was in his twenties and a student at Dartmouth College, left school to join the army. Franklin's family hero did so too. He was John McNeil, the huge, strapping husband of Franklin's older sister, Betsy. McNeil raised a company of men in Hillsborough and marched off to the war as a captain of militia. He served boldly and was wounded in the battle of Lundy's Lane. His heroism earned him a promotion. Just before the battle of Plattsburgh (Lake Champlain) in 1814, Franklin's brother John went off to fight. Franklin, then ten years old, wanted to go along with him. But his mother was firm and insisted that he would go to school and not to war. Franklin went to a brick schoolhouse at Hillsborough Center, a mile and a half from the house, and spent the war days dreaming behind his books. Shortly thereafter, the resources of the local school could no longer offer much to Franklin, and his father sent him to board at the Hancock Academy, a few miles farther on. Franklin grew homesick. He was just twelve years old when he went to Hancock, and he did not like being away from his family. One day he decided to go home. He slipped away from the school early on a Sunday morning and trudged homeward. He arrived at the big white house when everyone was at church and waited fearfully for his father to come home.

The general looked at his son and said nothing. They went in to Sunday dinner and talked of family things. It was just like always, and young Franklin was content.

But after dinner, the general had the carriage hitched up to his favorite horse. He beckoned to a quailing Franklin, who suddenly realized that he was being sent back to school. What is more, he was taught a lesson. The general took Franklin just halfway, then turned him out of the carriage and told him to walk the rest of the way back to the academy. It was a lesson in obedience which Franklin recalled in later life.

Yet it seems that the lesson did not take as well as it ought to have. For Franklin Pierce did not distinguish himself academically at Hancock. His father was not one to waste money, so there must have been some other reason to continue Franklin's education.

The general had sent his eldest boy, Benjamin, to Dartmouth. But after the war, he felt that Dartmouth had fallen into the hands of the Federalists (Daniel Webster was its most ardent advocate) and the general looked around for a school whose leader more typified his own Democratic-Republican political views. He found this leader in Dr. William Allen, who had been head of Dartmouth before he was ousted by the Federalists, and who went on to become President of Bowdoin

College in Brunswick, Maine. Franklin studied carefully at Francestown Academy so as to close up the deficiencies in his education. In the fall of 1820, his father and mother delivered the 16-year-old boy to Brunswick and placed him in the hands of President Allen.

First, there were entrance examinations at the house of President Allen. Franklin demonstrated that he could translate Greek and Latin, write a fair English hand, do arithmetic and that he knew his geography. He was matriculated, and began with 19 other students in the class of 1824. Dr. Allen recommended Mr. Grow's boardinghouse, and there the general and his wife took the boy and his trunk, and they left him to the loneliness of college life.

That life was strict in 1820. College was for learning and for little else. Here were the rules of Bowdoin:

No student shall eat or drink in any tavern unless in company with his parent or guardian, nor attend any theatrical entertainment or any idle show in Brunswick or Topsham, nor frequent any tavern or any house or shop after being forbidden by the President . . . Nor play at cards, billiards or any game of hazard nor at any game whatever for money or other things of value nor without permission keep a gun or pistol, nor discharge one nor go shooting or fishing.

No student shall be concerned in loud and disorderly singing in College, in shouting or clapping hands, nor in any Bacchanalian conduct disturbing the quietness, and dishonorable to the character of a literary institution.

No student may go out of town except into Topsham [the next town to Brunswick] nor be absent a night except by leave—upon request of parent or guardian.

Students must be in their rooms Saturday and Sunday evenings and abstain from diversions of every kind. They who profane the Sabbath by unnecessary business, visiting or receiving visits, or by walking abroad, or by any amusement, or in other ways, may be admonished or suspended.

The college consisted of three buildings, Massachusetts and Maine Halls, which were built of brick, and the chapel, which was wooden. Maine Hall was the student center where the upperclassmen lived and where most classes were held. (Massachusetts Hall was the science building and the house of the Bowdoin art collection.) The library was in the chapel but it was not of much use. It was open from 12 to 1 P.M. each day, and a freshman could only borrow one book every three weeks. Classes began with a bell that rang through Old Maine Hall at 8:30 in the morning. First there was an assembly conducted by President Allen. Recitations began at nine o'clock, then there was a study hour, followed by another recitation, dinner, an exercise period, study halls until late afternoon and finally one last recitation. The boys ate supper, went to evening prayer and then to their rooms to study until it was time for lights out. That first year, Franklin Pierce studied Xenophon, Livy and more arithmetic. The total cost for the year was about $200, which was a large amount of money in those days. Tuition was $24 a year, and room and board were about two dollars a week.

The family at home had high hopes for Franklin. His sisters wrote that he ought to conduct himself in a manner that would "merit the friendship and praise of all wise and virtuous people." But Franklin was not doing that. Freedom was a heady drug and he was captured by it. He spent many hours wandering in the cool, clean Maine woods and other hours in less acceptable pursuits—visiting an old woman who told fortunes with a pack of tattered cards or even frequenting the forbidden taverns.

At the end of the year, Franklin returned to Hillsborough for a vacation of four weeks, then went back to Bowdoin for his second year.

That year young Pierce was more outgoing and not as frightened as he had been when he first entered college. He "knew the ropes." He began to make friends; among them were young men such as Jonathan Cilley, Horatio Bridge and a shy fellow named Nathaniel Hawthorne. Another young man, Henry Wadsworth Longfellow, was a year behind this illustrious group, and so during Pierce's second year Longfellow was scarcely worth bothering about.

During his sophomore year, Pierce, along with several other students, lived at the home of a local dignitary. But the change of residence did not help his studies. He was frankly interested in "beating the system" and, at the end of the last term, found himself lowest man in the class scholastically.

The shock of this discovery came to Pierce during the first weeks of his third year, and it was like a bath of cold water. Suddenly, he realized that he was failing to do what his family expected of him. Furthermore, he had come under the influence of a deeply religious classmate named Zenas Caldwell, a devout Methodist, who would go on to join the ministry and become a powerful and famous New England preacher. With Caldwell's encouragement, Franklin Pierce set out to mend his academic ways. It was not an easy job, for bad study habits were not easily changed to good ones. He found difficulty in concentrating; it was too easy to allow a buzzing fly or an outside noise to break his train of thought.

Earlier, Pierce had been very much the gay scamp. One day, when he was asked the solution to a difficult problem in algebra, he rattled off the answer in a way that surprised the instructor, who knew that Pierce seldom studied his lessons.

"How did you get this solution?" asked the instructor.

"From Stowe's slate," Pierce replied.

But that was in the sophomore year—a sophomoric trick. In his junior year, Pierce was a new student. He became chapel monitor, and the discipline of attending chapel every day carried over to his studies. He no longer missed a recitation or came to class unprepared as he had done so many times before.

During one vacation, Pierce went home with Zenas Caldwell and apparently profited from the powerful atmosphere of religious devotion he found in the house. His will to succeed was strengthened. He spent several weeks teaching in a local school at a salary of $14 a month and then went back to Bowdoin. This year, he was a leader in many ways. It was long before the days of ROTC, but Pierce and his friends formed a military company of students, and Pierce was elected captain. He led the marches, while a clumsy Nathaniel Hawthorne— Private Hawthorne—marched in the rear rank.

During the summer vacation between his junior and senior years at Bowdoin, Pierce remained at the college to study. Here was an indication of the grave change that had come over him during the year. He had the privilege of living in Main Hall during his senior year with Caldwell as his roommate. He was elected chairman of the Athenean Literary Society. When the year ended in a blaze of honors for those who deserved them, Pierce found that he had risen from last man to fifth in his class. He was asked to make a commencement oration. His one disappointment was that his father could not come to the ceremonies which were held at Bowdoin late in the summer. The general was otherwise occupied with the Marquis de Lafayette, the French hero of the American Revolution, who had come to pay a visit to the country which was nearly as dear to him as his native France. The general, as the leading representative of the old Revolutionary warriors, had to be on hand in Portsmouth for the welcoming ceremonies. So Pierce was graduated without his family to share his triumph.

2

THE
LOCAL
POLITICIAN

Franklin Pierce was graduated from Bowdoin College in the summer of 1824. The second administration of James Monroe was coming to an end. Monroe's years in office were known as "the Era of Good Feeling," largely because the Federalist party had died out in most of the states, and the majority of politicians espoused the cause of the Democratic-Republicans. The name of the "Era" was misleading. There was as much political difference in the country as ever, but it was factional difference rather than party difference. The Pierces had the same political friends and the same political enemies, but they came under different hats these days.

There was no military cause in 1824 to attract the service of a young college graduate and, with his education, Pierce had fitted himself out for public life. There was one thing to be done: to acquaint himself sufficiently with the laws of the land so that he might be accepted before the bar. Such practice was common in those days, for a politician needed a way of making a living, and law was the most suitable.

General Pierce had secured the paying office of postmaster

of Hillsborough, and he turned the job over to Franklin when the young man came home from Bowdoin. Franklin Pierce delivered the mail, sold stamps and began the study of law under the tutelage of a local lawyer named John Burnham. It was a busy fall; one filled with politicking. General Pierce's hero, Andrew Jackson, the heir to the Democratic-Republican leadership, was running for President against a large field of candidates which included Henry Clay, the very popular William H. Crawford and John Quincy Adams.

The fall elections did not produce a winner; Clay and Jackson and Crawford and Adams were still all in the running. But Crawford fell ill and lost his chance. In the end, it came down to a choice of Jackson or John Quincy Adams, and Clay threw his support to Adams for the latter's victory.

The election was discouraging for the Pierces. They knew the Adamses as old Federalists, and no matter what protestations John Quincy Adams might make, General Pierce and his son did not trust the Massachusetts man a whit. General Pierce had some political ambitions of his own these days, and the election of an opposition man to the presidency did not help.

The postmastership, of course, would not last now that political opponents were in federal office, and Franklin Pierce discovered there were too many diversions at his father's house to study law properly. He went to Portsmouth in the spring of 1825, where he could concentrate as a clerk sitting in the law offices of Levi Woodbury, an old family friend. He began a stern routine, arising at 5:30 in the morning and studying until 11 o'clock at night. For the first few months, at least, he did not go out in the evenings and did not even visit acquaintances during the day.

In 1826, General Pierce was named by local politicians in several parts of New Hampshire as a possible candidate for governor. His candidacy was backed by those who disliked John Quincy Adams most. Pierce ran and was defeated by 5,000 votes. The election brought the family into greater prominence in the state. Two years later, General Pierce was elected governor of New Hampshire and appeared at his Inauguration in his old three-cornered hat—the symbol of the Revolutionary soldier—to the cheers of the people. The term was only a year then. The duties were largely ceremonial, for New Hampshiremen preferred to keep control of lawmaking in the hands of the legislature. But the honor was great.

That same year, 1827, Franklin Pierce completed his law study, and in September he was admitted to practice before the bar of New Hampshire. The general built an office across the road from the house, and Franklin Pierce hung out his shingle as a lawyer. He began to take an active interest in political and civic affairs. One day he led a parade in honor of Jackson's victory at New Orleans and made a speech which was highly applauded at the banquet. From time to time, he was selected as chairman of a town meeting, usually to espouse the Democratic-Republican cause in one way or another.

As a politician, Franklin Pierce was showing himself to be very effective. As a lawyer, he was not so proud of himself. When spring came, he rode to Amherst, the county seat, to try the cases that had been worked up during the winter. Unfortunately he lost his first case. It was a serious disappointment to the young lawyer, but he took it in his stride. "I will try nine hundred and ninety-nine cases if clients will continue to trust me," he said. "And if I fail, just as I have today, I will try the thousandth." It did not take nearly that long before he began to win cases. Yet, as Nathaniel Hawthorne recorded in his biography of Pierce, when Hawthorne came to visit the young lawyer and politician at about this time, he noted that Pierce was far more interested in politics than in his law business.

Politics required a good deal of his time, if he was to be successful. "The Era of Good Feeling" was far behind. The enmity between the supporters of the Adamses and those of

Jackson was out in the open, and it led to bitter arguments and often to physical violence. Oddly enough, however, the political activity brought law business to Franklin Pierce that he would otherwise never have seen, for those who supported him politically wanted to do something for him.

In January, 1828, his law business amounted to as much as it had been in all the previous six months. In May, his political activity brought him an appointment as justice of the peace and more income. He was also elected by his townsmen as their representative at the state legislature in the Great and General Court, as the lawmaking body was then called. Of course, the victory of the Democratic-Republicans was nearly complete, for Andrew Jackson had won over Adams in the election of 1828. And up from the backwoods to Concord came Franklin Pierce. He was to become the only son of a governor of the Granite State ever to serve in the legislature while his father held the state's highest office.

So at 24, young Franklin Pierce came to the state capital at Concord to represent his 2,000 townsmen as state legislator. His political career was well begun.

There were 239 members of the General Court in those days, and their arrival at the sleepy little capital turned it from a dull place to a bright one, overnight. Many of the backwoods legislators were hard-drinking men who slept in their boots and trousers, and sometimes Franklin had a tendency (which he himself lamented) to join the roisterers and drink more than he should. He was on good behavior at the opening of the legislature, however, because it would never do for the governor's son to disgrace his family name or that of the state. Governor and legislator, father and son, went to stay at John George's house near the old North Church. They each paid fifty cents a day for board and room.

Franklin arrived first. His father would come in the middle of the week and would be greeted by as much pageantry as New

Hampshire was capable of giving and was inclined to bestow. This year, the Jacksonian Democrats were very firmly in power, and so a comfortable feeling prevailed among the Pierces and their supporters. There was opposition to General Pierce, of course (some hoped to avert his final approval by the Great and General Court), but nothing came of it except a little prelegislative excitement. The general was duly inaugurated for a new term and the 30 day session of the legislature began. New Hampshiremen were frugal in their government expenses; they did not keep a legislature in session any longer than was necessary. They did not allow it to pass any laws infringing on individual rights unless it could be deemed essential to the general welfare—and proof of this was hard to establish.

And what were the needs they accepted in 1829? For one thing, the state needed new roads, if the farmers were to get their crops to the market and seeds to their farms.

And what should be done about education? A tax had been levied earlier for educational use, but who was to get the money? Some wanted it distributed to the various towns to support their public schools. Others wanted to establish a state university. Governor Pierce was one of the leaders in favor of the university, and Franklin also wanted to back the plan, for both felt that Dartmouth College, the major state institution, was far too lordly and "Federalist" inclined.

As a young man and a first-term legislator, it was best for Franklin Pierce to be silent and speak when called upon. Yet he had one great advantage—he was one of the few men in the legislature with a college education. So he was chosen, in spite of his youth and inexperience, to head the Committee on Education. As chairman, he led an investigation into the management of primary education by the towns of the state. The knotty question before the legislature was whether education should be managed by a general committee from each town, or by committees in the school districts into which each town

was divided. Legislator Pierce and his colleagues decided on
the latter course as the most representative of the people. As
Jacksonian Democrats, they were constantly measuring legislative ideas against the independence of the electorate. As for the
matter of the university—it was far too weighty for quick
consideration and decision.

Franklin Pierce made his first speech in the legislature on
the subject of the press and who should publish the laws passed
by the legislature. Most of the papers were anti-Jackson, so he
naturally spoke up for limiting the publication of the laws, for
which the state paid as advertising. His idea and that of his
friends was to limit publication of the laws to the Jackson
newspapers. He spoke up for the measure and was pleased
when it passed. Actually, many others spoke for and against the
measure, but young Pierce had been "baptized" as a legislator
that day. His talk of economy and his use of language were very
impressive to his constituents. He stood on "high principle"
but, of course, all his legislative compatriots knew that the issue
was not only one of high principle but also practical politics.
It was, and would always be, Pierce's mark as a politician that
he found a high principle to back his most pragmatic actions.

Aside from attending the sessions of the legislature, Franklin
Pierce made himself very well-known and quite popular among
the Jacksonian Democrats. The Jacksonian Democrats were
gradually dropping the name Democratic-Republican and
eventually became the Democratic party of the 20th century.
Every night, the Jackson supporters met at the governor's
lodgings or at the Eagle Coffee House to discuss political affairs
and the best ways of bringing victory to their cause and political poverty to the enemy. Sometimes they met at the house of
Isaac Hill, the most prominent editor of the *Patriot*, the New
Hampshire voice of Jacksonism. Isaac Hill was President Jackson's most important advisor in New England, and by watch-

ing him in action, young Franklin Pierce learned much about practical politics.

The session was over; those miraculous 30 days passed much too quickly. Soon the Pierces went home to Hillsborough. But Franklin was not satisfied. He had seen the capital, he had been excited by the motion of politics, and being stuck away in this backwoods village bored him. He went back to Concord for a special session in June, and then the thought of settling down was even harder to bear. He found an excuse to go away on a trip; his older brother Sullivan and his wife had both died in Detroit. Someone was needed to go and bring the two little girls, who had been orphaned, back to the family. Franklin promptly undertook the journey and spent six weeks traveling to the West by way of Saratoga, Utica and Buffalo. When he came back, he was busy for a time, but not so busy that he could not take a trip to Boston that same year.

He spent the winter in Hillsborough—a long winter in which the roads were often made so impassable by snow that the farmers did not go out except to feed the stock and milk the cows. Franklin Pierce was bored. He wrote his brother-in-law, John McNeil, who was in Boston and lamented about his confinement to the backwoods. "I want something in an hour of relaxation besides trudging from house to the office and back again," he said. "I should like some society which might keep off that *ennui* so sure to punish a moment of idleness—something to break the dull monotony which, in such a place as this, hangs about human existence."

But if Franklin Pierce did not have excitement that winter, he did see his political fortunes improved. At the annual town meeting, he was chosen moderator for the third time, and once again he was selected as the town's legislator.

General Pierce's term as governor had expired in 1830. Now in his seventies, he was happy to step down for younger men. He returned to Hillsborough that year, an honored citizen among New Hampshiremen. Franklin then continued to carry the political honors for the family. In the session of 1830, the Jacksonians were again in power, and this time young Pierce learned something about "gerrymandering," or the art of changing political boundaries to put the "right" voters in the "right" places. He had been made chairman of the Committee on Towns and Parishes. His friends pointed out that, some years earlier, the Adams men had created the town of Franklin next to Northfield, in order to take assets from Democratic Northfield and give then to Federalists who lived in Franklin. Pierce tried to change this and found that he was voted down, almost unanimously, by his own committee. But he carried the issue—to restore to Northfield its property—and eventually won the fight on the open floor of the House. He gained much honor, and some political enemies, in doing so. He certainly gained experience in the hurly-burly of practical politics.

In 1831, Franklin Pierce was sent back to the legislature once again, and that year he was nominated to be speaker of the House, the greatest honor it could offer. He was elected, too, and at the age of 26 was presiding over 229 legislators. He bought a frock coat, wore a big tie and made a fine figure on the podium. His friends called him "a devilish fine speaker" and his enemies simply compared him to the devil. He was full of laughter and smiles that year, but he also knuckled down to the hard task of presiding over a body of men of many different views. And that same year, he was appointed military aide to Governor Samuel Dinsmoor. It was only an honorary title, but Franklin was delighted at being called "Colonel Pierce" after that. He still harked back, secretly, to those old days when he had sat at his father's knee and heard the stirring stories of the Revolution. Had his life been different, he would indeed have chosen to be a soldier instead of a political leader with a soldier's title.

3

CONGRESSMAN

In 1832, New Hampshire was solidly behind President Andrew Jackson and his domestic policies of conservative management. The general's approach appealed to New Hampshiremen because the farmers of this rockbound New England state have always believed in stern business policies, in saving money and in the avoidance of debt. Thus, there was virtually no opposition to Andrew Jackson in the spring of 1832, after he was renominated for the presidency at Baltimore. Nor was there any opposition to Franklin Pierce—a leading Jacksonian—and he returned to Concord that year as a representative from Hillsborough.

He very nearly did not return—but that was personal, not political. Pierce was almost killed in a youthful prank which showed his ebullience, but which did not reflect much credit on his military judgment. When the news of the renomination of Jackson reached Hillsborough, Pierce and the other Jacksonians in town threw up their hats and cheered. Was that enough celebration? Apparently it was not, so they found an old four-pounder cannon left over from the Revolutionary days and decided to fire it. Long before, the cannon had lost its carriage. All they had was the long metal tube with its muzzle at one end and the touchhole at the other end. What they needed was a gun carriage but there was none to be found in peaceful Hillsborough that spring of 1832. A bright fellow among the crowd of cronies came forth with a pair of wooden cartwheels and an axle. The gun was chained securely to the axle, and then, pushing and tugging, the friends hauled it up to the top of the Meeting House Hill, where the Liberty Pole stood. Around this pole in spring, the children danced in celebration of American independence, and on Fourth of July it was decorated with bunting. It was the center of all patriotic activity, and the renomination of Jackson, said the friends that day, was certainly patriotic enough.

The principle of an ancient cannon was the same as the principle of a modern big gun; for every action there is a direct and equal reaction. (Franklin Pierce seems to have forgotten his physics.) The old cannons were mounted on slides so that when they were fired, their guns would slide back, forced by the reaction from the muzzle blast. But that day, the excited young politicians had their gun chained down to the axles. So when they fired it, in honor of General Jackson, the gun exploded, and Franklin Pierce was very lucky to come away with his arms and legs intact.

A few days later, undaunted, Pierce went to Concord, where he was quickly caught up in new excitement. He was elected speaker of the House once again, and it was almost unanimous. Only three of the nearly 300 legislators opposed him. During that year came a new honor: Pierce was selected, along with four others, to put up a slate of candidates for various offices, from governor to congressional representative.

Pierce was popular—the newspapers called him the most popular man in New Hampshire—and he was selected as the congressional nominee himself. Politics being what they were that year, designation was almost equal to election, but he campaigned all summer for Andrew Jackson in New Hampshire and Massachusetts, and then was elected himself. His father, the benign old general, was chosen to be a presidential elector, which meant he would go to Washington and cast his vote for his favorite, General Andrew Jackson. It was a grand year for the Pierces; perhaps just a little bit dull, because there was virtually no opposition. Speaker Pierce wrote to a friend saying that the affairs of the House were dull, because there was no voice of dissent. In the votes for Congress, for example, although some of the old Federalist-thinking newspaper editors had put up a handful of candidates, the five men chosen by the legislature (all Jacksonians) won election very handily, averaging 23,000 votes each to about 5,000 for their opponents.

In the spring of 1833, Franklin Pierce had planned to make a long trip around the United States before going to Washington and settling down for the coming congressional session. But cholera struck the Eastern seaboard that spring and put an end to all his plans. Cholera! It was a dreaded disease which plagued the America of the 1830's. The year before cholera had hit New York, causing hundreds of cases a day. The public health authorities did not know how the disease spread, and the frightened public virtually deserted the city that summer. It was the same, in 1833, in both Connecticut and Massachusetts. Everyone who could flee to the country left the cities, and the steamboats and ships were loaded with people escaping their neighbors. That summer, Franklin Pierce did go to Boston to visit his sister Betsy and her husband John McNeil and, while there, he came down with an ailment that was suspiciously like cholera. They called it a "bilious attack," which meant that he became very sick and vomited—as did the cholera victims—so strenuously that for a time there was fear that he might die. But he recovered, and by autumn was well enough to make the difficult journey from New Hampshire to Washington.

In 1833, this was a very hard trip. Franklin Pierce rode to Boston by coach, and then took another to one of the ports on Long Island Sound where a steamboat would take him to New York City. The steamboats sometimes ran around Cape Cod, but few ventured to go far out at sea; they simply were not built for such travel in those early days. From New York, Congressman Pierce took another steamboat to Amboy, New Jersey, and there boarded one of the cars of the New Amboy and Camden railroad which had begun operating at the end of 1832. From Amboy, the cars carried him at 18 miles an hour —record speed then—to Bordentown, where he took a steamboat down the Delaware, arriving at Philadelphia on the third night after leaving Boston. From Philadelphia, he took another boat to New Castle, Delaware, another rail journey to Frenchtown, a steamboat to Baltimore, and then a coach ride of 40 miles to the capital of Washington.

In a few days, Congressman Pierce was established at Mrs. Hill's boardinghouse on Pennsyvlania Avenue, near Third Street. It was a four-story brick house, kept in Southern style, with a dozen Negro servants who blacked the boots of the lodgers and did their bidding. They were slaves, of course, and this was Franklin Pierce's first encounter with slavery. If Pierce was struck by his introduction to this institution, he did not give any indication of it. He simply observed that the Negroes sang a lot and seemed to go about their work cheerfully enough.

These "messes" represented the common manner in which senators and congressmen lived. Few were so bold as to build houses for themselves. There was a shortage of housing in Washington, but legislators were not so certain of their longevity that they would waste money. Furthermore, most of them lived so far from Washington, and the journey was so arduous that families often did not come to the capital at all. The legislators would arrive in the late autumn, Congress would convene, usually around December 1, and would remain in session until March, when most of the work would be complete. The legislators then went home, to return the following December.

On December 2, 1833, Franklin Pierce officially became the representative of New Hampshire—the youngest man in the delegation—and settled down to work. As a very junior representative, Pierce was fortunate to find himself granted a seat on the important Judiciary Committee. Every day, then, Pierce braved the dust or mud of the unpaved Pennsylvania Avenue, to catch a ride in a carriage or a horse-drawn jitney bus that stopped at every corner, picking up passengers. He went to the Capitol, where the north wing housed the Senate, with the Supreme Court in the basement, the Library of Congress on the west front, and the House of Representatives in the south wing in a semicircular room surrounded by marble pillars.

The first order of business was to organize the House and then to hear what President Jackson had to say in his State of the Union message. This speech would indicate the direction he hoped Congress would take in the coming months. Congressman Pierce listened to the message with full enthusiasm. He agreed with President Jackson that the National Bank was a monstrosity, best eliminated when its charter expired, and that it should not be supported until that time by the government's money. But others did not agree, and the first weeks of the session were almost entirely taken up by the National Bank question. On each roll call, Congressman Pierce voted the Jackson position and, eventually, late in February, the question of depositing money in the National Bank was referred to the Ways and Means Committee of the House, where it might easily die.

On February 27, 1833, Franklin Pierce made his first speech

in Congress on the subject of Revolutionary pensions. Many old fighters as well as their widows and orphans were making claims against the government. For several years, the usual way of making a claim had been to bring up a private bill "for the relief of so and so. . . ." There were so many congressmen with private bills that the leadership had decided to make a law covering the general subject. But Franklin Pierce felt that since the Revolutionary War had ended long ago, all the just claims had been settled, and he arose to speak against a special bill for Revolutionary War payments. He spoke for three-quarters of an hour and earned much applause, even from such crusty figures as John Quincy Adams, with whom Pierce disagreed, in principle, on almost everything.

That speech was the highlight of the session for the young New Hampshire congressman. Otherwise, he was immersed in a swirl of detail, for the kind of business that came before the Judiciary Committee involved claims by people and governments, patent renewals, and everything relating to the courts and their relationship with Congress. Pierce had no secretary and no office. He worked at his desk in the House of Representatives or in his room at Mrs. Hill's boardinghouse. He wrote his own papers and letters with a stiff quill pen. He got up before eight o'clock and had breakfast at nine. Then he went to the House or to one of the government departments, if he was transacting business for some constituent. He usually appeared for committee hearings and carried on correspondence until noon when the House met, in sessions that lasted three or four hours. There was no break for lunch, but a hungry young man could adjourn to the oyster bar in the basement of the House for a snack to hold him until the next real meal, which was dinner served at Mrs. Hill's late in the afternoon. The final meal was a light supper served after dark.

That was Franklin Pierce's routine. There were amusements, beginning with the President's reception on New Year's

Day. Some senators and congressmen gave parties. There was the theater. There were excursions in hot weather, up the Potomac, or the Chesapeake and Ohio Canal. As for work, the Congress did lay on the table the matter of the deposits of the National Bank, as might have been expected from a Jacksonian House. As far as Pierce was concerned, he began to show a certain independence of mind here. In spite of Jacksonians, he voted against giving settlers on public lands automatic rights to those lands. He also voted against various internal improvements, even though Jackson had accepted the idea. In a way, one could say that Pierce was out-Jacksoning Jackson; he went back to the old Jeffersonian days for his principles. He believed the federal government should be limited in its powers, and he did not want those powers extended. "Let the states take care of such matters as internal improvements and the granting of lands," he said.

In the summer, Franklin Pierce came home to find that his conduct had been generally approved by the people of New Hampshire, and they had nominated him for a second term in office. In the end, Jackson had been upheld on the National Bank issue. The real result of this issue was the emergence of the Whig coalition to oppose Jackson and to strengthen the party system again, after a period of quiescence. Franklin Pierce could not have been more unconcerned. He had voted as he was expected to do and as his conscience had led him. Thus, he had earned the second-term designation—not an empty honor in New Hampshire, where few men were sent back to Washington a second time, and practically never was a man given a third term. Independent New Hampshiremen did not like the idea of entrenching power. Their sense of republicanism was very strong.

Franklin Pierce joined his fellows in a dislike of show, but he was dedicated now to a political life. That year, he felt more at home in politics than before and was prepared to commit

Jane Means Appleton Pierce, wife of Franklin Pierce

himself to a future. That future included a wife, Jane Means Appleton, whom he had met sometime before. She was the daughter of the former President of Bowdoin College, and they were often brought together in her Massachusetts home by mutual friends, including an old teacher of Pierce's from the Bowdoin days. They were married in November, 1834, just before Pierce had to go back to Washington for the next session of Congress. Whether or not Jane would go was debatable, for she was slender and shy and was known to have tuberculosis. But she wanted to go and, being a girl of strong will, she did go. Just after the wedding in Amherst, they set out for the capital, and after staying at Brown's Indian Queen Inn for one night, they settled at Birth's boardinghouse for the winter.

Jane Pierce was an excellent wife to Franklin Pierce, because she was everything that he was not. She came from an old, sheltered New England family with its roots around Boston. She was, in short, an aristocrat with aristocratic ideas, while he was a frontier egalitarian, very rough in his ways and full of high spirits that needed taming. She had much to teach him in the way of manners, and he was very willing to learn, for he was a very ambitious young man.

That year, there was not much food for his ambition, insofar as making a name for himself in Washington was concerned. He did serve on a committee that investigated the educational system at the United States Military Academy at West Point. Too many cadets were securing free education from Uncle Sam and resigning their commissions after graduation. As a militiaman and the son of a militiaman, Pierce had little use for the "spit and polish" officers of the regular army, but he made little headway in airing his dislikes on this occasion. The committee split, and the minority managed to exert enough influence in the House to suppress the critical report of the majority.

The session ended March 4, although all the business of

Congress was not finished. But the senators and representatives got itchy to go home about that time. Why they should have been so eager that year was odd, since the rivers were frozen over and the Northern Congressmen, at least, would have to wait for more clement weather before going home. While the Pierces were still in the South, the congressional election was held in connection with the town meetings, and Pierce was returned again, although he did not learn about it until later.

He decided to settle near his own home, and bought a house in Hillsborough. Mrs. Pierce stopped off with relatives in Boston that spring, while he went ahead to fix up the house for her. Then, in May, she joined him to find that he had put in gravel walks, fences and new wallpaper. The spring and summer months were spent putting the affairs of the house and the farm in order and settling back into the law business.

That summer, a young man named Albert Baker came to live with General Pierce and study law with Franklin. The young man was the brother of Mary Baker Eddy, who would found the Christian Science movement, and her brother became the mainstay of the Pierce law office, during the time Franklin was in Washington. In the fall—it was 1834 now—Franklin set out again for Washington and the House of Representatives. Mrs. Pierce had not found Washington to her liking. It was too rough and dirty for her, and her health was not so robust that she could travel easily. They decided, therefore, that Jane would spend the winter visiting friends and relatives. Colonel Pierce, as Franklin now styled himself, and his wife went to Boston, where he saw her safely settled with relatives. Then, he left for Washington.

In this session of Congress, which began on December 1, 1835, Pierce was lucky for one of his friends became speaker of the House. The friend was James K. Polk of Tennessee, and that friendship was to be both an indicator of Franklin Pierce's beliefs and instrumental in hardening those beliefs. The fact was that Pierce was more than a little annoyed and disturbed by the rising tide of Abolitionism that was moving on Washington. He did not believe in the right of preachers, or others, in New Hampshire and Boston to try and promote social change in the Southern states. What the people of any state did, he said, was their own business. Basically, this position came from Pierce's belief in the doctrine of states' rights, which he had espoused as a child. What seemed important to him in the days when the Federalists were claiming the right to dam rivers and build roads anywhere in the Union, seemed important now in a different way. One might quarrel with Pierce's position on slavery, as it developed in those days, but one could not quarrel with the consistency of his logic in arriving at the position. The doctrine of states' rights was an important matter. Had the states not agreed to limit the power of the federal government back in the days of the formation of the Constitution, there would have been no Union. To be sure, the Union was developing and changing, but the strict constructionists, such as Pierce, did not want it to change in the matter of the rights of the people to govern themselves at the lowest and most local level. Among the American Presidents who had to face the slavery issue at the time of crisis, two were definitely ruled by the same set of principles: Pierce and Buchanan. Both of these men had many Southern friends and felt drawn to the political position of the South. Without being slaveowners, with no hypocrisy or thought of personal or sectional gain, they honestly took positions on the states' rights issue, refusing to go the higher moral route and accept the need for change to eliminate slavery.

Speaker Polk did what political leaders have always done. He chose men that he trusted and liked to be around him, and so young Franklin Pierce was selected to serve on several special committees of Congress that year, and his reputation was enhanced. Pierce's friendship with Polk, of course, strengthened the views that he shared with him—and Polk was a Southern slaveholder and a Jacksonian who was wedded to the concept of states' rights.

Slavery had been an American ulcer for many years, but in the 1830's, the issue was pressed more vigorously by the Abolitionists. There were several reasons. Britain had outlawed her slave trade and was making serious efforts to suppress the trade north of the equator. (It was more or less agreed that the Spanish and Portuguese might continue their trade in the South, that is, in the Latin American countries they controlled.) Slavery had proved uneconomic and antisocial in the Northern states. Thus, when the preachers, and the good ladies and the editors of the North spoke out against slavery, it was easy for them to do so because it was not a Northern problem. No businessman with dollars invested rose to challenge them in the name of good old American enterprise. The antislavery movement gained strength in the North and brought a new cohesion to the moralists. Abolition, churchgoing and temperance were almost always found under the same political roof. Since 1820, the ladies and their allies had been fulminating and, except for the South, which was the unhappy object of the argument, little attention was paid to the problems the argument was causing on a national scale. One reason for this was the Missouri Compromise which had temporarily settled the political issue of slavery. Now, however, shadows were on the horizon. People were beginning to think about Texas as a new state; and Texas, breaking away from Mexico, was slave territory. There was also contemplation of other areas in the Southwest and Northwest. Had Pierce been a high intellectual, he might have reconsidered his position in the light of Jackson's changing attitude toward states' rights. The huge change for Jackson came in 1832, when, as President, he was compelled to take issue with South Carolina's refusal to obey the national tax laws (nullification of the tariff). He threatened to use force to make this state accept federal authority. Actually, as America grew, it became apparent that the old doctrine of states' rights was not conducive to a reasonable and moral growth of the Union, but Pierce, like millions of others, was unable to free himself of his childhood beliefs.

Thus, in December, 1835, when 172 ladies of Maine presented a petition to Representative John Fairfield, which he offered to Congress on December 16, Pierce and others regarded the move with distaste. Fairfield's petition was offered under the specific right of the people to petition Congress for redress of grievances. The grievance of the ladies was that slavery in the District of Columbia was an abomination to all Americans who hated slavery, and since the District was a federal property, not a state, Congress had the right to regulate slavery there as well as the moral obligation to wipe it out.

The petition of the ladies might not have aroused very much emotion in Congress, except that it came at a very bad time. The Southern states were becoming very sensitive about slavery, especially in view of the Jacksonian position on federal power. To Southern thinkers, the Nullification Issue of 1832 had never been settled. South Carolina had backed down when Jackson had indicated he would push a force bill through Congress. When it was done over the South's objections, South Carolina had made haste to obey the law and thus sidetracked the issue, but not without clouds of rhetoric. In 1835, Georgians became very sensitive about the criticism of slavery. The Abolitionists were flooding the South with propaganda. The slaveowners found that the propaganda appealed to some townsfolk who did not have slaves, and it made the slaves harder to handle as they became aware that there were people in the North who wanted their freedom. In 1835, Georgia passed a new law providing a death penalty to anyone who published material tending to incite slave insurrections. Under the law, thousands of ladies and preachers and Abolitionists would have been punished had they lived in the South.

Everywhere in the South that summer, Abolitionist agitators were put into wagons and onto trains and shipped to the North. Some were tarred and feathered. Others were beaten. The South was very angry, and of course, when abused agitators returned to the North and appeared at public meetings to tell of their misadventures, the Northern Abolitionists became even more determined to put an end to slavery in the South. In Charleston harbor, a whole boatload of Abolitionist tracts was seized that summer and burned in a public orgy of hatred against the "do-gooders." Alfred Huger, the postmaster of Charleston, asked Washington to put an end to the mailing of Abolitionist propaganda to the South, but the Postmaster General in Washington said he had no authority to bar this propaganda from the mails. On December 2, when Andrew Jackson made his State of the Nation Address to Congress, he had suggested a law to bar antislavery material in the mails, but this had simply caused the Southern and Northern congressmen and senators to line up on the sides of their own views and constituents.

John Fairfield's petition came then, just two weeks after the issue began to boil in Washington. It was a very bad time.

Franklin Pierce was faced with a problem. There were many Abolitionists in New Hampshire, and he knew it. The famous English Abolitionist, George Thompson, had been invited to speak there that very summer. George Thompson came, and he drew a hearty crowd when he spoke. But George Thompson was also booed loudly, and hit by several rotten eggs thrown from the back of the crowd. So there it was: Even in New Hampshire, Abolition divided the people. Pierce knew that as well as anyone, and yet he was quite disgusted with the Abolitionists and their excesses. "I do not believe there is one person out of a hundred who does not wholly reprobate the course of the few reckless fanatics who are able only to disturb occasionally the quiet of a village," he wrote to Speaker Polk. And Congressman Pierce honestly believed that the Abolitionists of his home state were weak, not only in number, but in their grasp upon the imagination of the people. In mid-December he arose in the House and spoke to that effect. "There is not the slightest disposition to interfere with any rights secured by the Constitution, which binds together this great and glorious Confederacy as one family," he said then, again assuring Congress that New Hampshiremen detested the Abolitionists as he did.

But there was a strong Abolition movement in New Hampshire centered in Concord, and that movement had its own newspaper, *The Herald of Freedom*. Pierce's words and his stand were attacked in the paper. When John C. Calhoun arose in the Senate and attacked the Northerners for their views on slavery, Isaac Hill, the senator from New Hampshire condemned Calhoun for the attack. In his own defense, Calhoun picked up a copy of *The Herald of Freedom*, which attacked Pierce for a statement he had made that not one in 500 New Hampshiremen supported Abolition. The editor printed a petition signed by "more than one in 500" of local people to prove his point. Pierce was aghast and upset that he was being called a liar, and that his good name was being dragged through the depths of this argument. He answered Calhoun in the House, and the argument went on. It was a good indication—this emotionalism of Calhoun and of Pierce —of what the Abolition issue was doing to all the people. Pierce thought Calhoun was calling him a liar. Calhoun was trying to use all the ammunition possible to show the danger he felt from the North. And everybody seemed to be misunderstanding the motives of everybody else. Pierce became so incensed before it was finished that he offered to duel anyone who thought the article in the New Hampshire paper was true and that he told lies.

One reason for Pierce's extreme sensitivity at this time was poor health. He suffered from a nagging cold all that winter. Another reason was his state of mind. A baby, Franklin, Jr., was born on February 2, 1836, but the baby died three days later. Pierce learned that his wife Jane was not rallying well in Massachusetts after the hurt and disappointment of losing a child. His family worries and his health also may have contributed to an episode that became something of a scandal. In those days there was a good deal of excessive drinking among congressmen, as there was among the populace, particularly in the frontier areas such as those where Pierce lived. One night Pierce and Congressmen Henry Wise of Virginia and Edward Hannegan of Indiana spent too many hours with a bottle before deciding to go to the theater. At the theater, they found they were sharing a box with an army officer with whom Hannegan had quarreled earlier. Hannegan drew a gun, and soon the theater was in an uproar. The result was an unpleasant scandal that was exposed by the newspapers. Pierce also fell ill from his carousal and ended up in bed with a case of pleurisy. It was the second week of March before he was in good health again and able to attend to his congressional work.

He came back to a Congress that was wracked with more dissension than any in history. The full force of the Abolition movement was being exerted against the dissenters who did not want the issue of slavery tampered with by Congress. Two pointed issues came before the nation at that time, and the Congress could not ignore them. First was the success of the rebellion of Texas against Mexico, which aroused the fears of the Abolitionists that Texas would seek and be granted admission to the Union as a slave state. Second, and much more vital to Congress at that moment, was the committee report on the question of Abolition, petitions and slavery in federal territories. The Pinckney Committee had studied the question of petitions and had come to the conclusion that petitions urging

Congress to end slavery would be accepted by Congress, only to be immediately laid on the table and never acted upon. From the distance of a century and a quarter, one can see that this solution was no solution. It would never do for Congress to give up its power, to deny that it could and must act one way or the other on the legitimate demands of Americans. But, in 1835, this decision seemed a way out of an intolerable situation. Pierce quite agreed with the committee report and joined the majority of congressmen in voting for it. One might say that Pierce was seared by this session of Congress, and that his views on the suppression of slavery were set then. But Pierce's politics also went back farther; they represented the frontier and the knowledge he acquired from his father, to say nothing of the old general's prejudices.

The last week of this session of Congress was a nightmare. Friend stood against friend, and animosity filled the corridors of the Houses. The slavery issue permeated every cranny.

On the one side, John Quincy Adams and other Abolitionists were fulminating against the Pinckney Committee report and the final legislative suggestion, which would go down in history as the Gag Rule.

On the other hand, Texas was beginning to stir with demands for annexation to the United States, and her supporters in Congress were moving. John Quincy Adams led the fight in the House against Texas' annexation, too, because he said the addition of a slave state was anathema to the North. The Gag Rule passed, 117 to 68, and the rioting began. At the end of May, bills came up calling for the introduction of Michigan and Arkansas as states, and fights broke out in the press gallery. The bills passed, but only in an atmosphere of half-carnival, half-battlefield. Pierce had an honor bestowed on him, if one could call it that; part of the time he occupied the speaker's chair as speaker *pro tem*, in the absence of Polk. As June came on, the congressmen became anxious to go home and mend fences because they were sick of the growing heat in Washington. But speakers and issues still kept them there. Pierce gave his anti-West Point speech during the debate on the appropriations bills. It did him no good to complain about the lax spirit of young men educated for the army, who then went off to civilian employment. In a way it seemed that everyone in Congress that spring was talking at the top of his lungs and no one was listening. Perhaps this is what happens in time of crisis everywhere, and crisis was most certainly the prevailing atmosphere in all of Washington in the spring of 1836. It finally ended, and Congressman Franklin Pierce wearily closed up his desk and headed home for New Hampshire's green mountains.

4

SENATOR

During that spring of 1836, Franklin Pierce was passed over by New Hampshiremen as they decided on the new members of Congress. It was a little confusing—the election was held in the spring of 1836, but for a Congress that would begin to work in 1837. Thus, although he was not reelected, Pierce was obligated to go back to Washington in the fall of 1836 and stay there until March 4, 1837. The reason for Pierce's apparent failure was hardly a disgrace. His friends let the congressional seat go by because they were seeking the senate seat for Pierce. So Pierce went back, apparently a loser, and Jane went with him. She was hardly ever well, however, and spent most of her time in seclusion. Pierce made a number of new friends, including Jefferson Davis of Mississippi, who had appeared on the Washington scene. But such friendship seemed ephemeral, for Pierce half expected to retire to New Hampshire in the spring and spend the rest of his years as a lawyer-farmer.

He went to Washington with those thoughts in mind, but almost before he arrived, the state legislature met and elected

Pierce United States Senator for the full six-year term, beginning March 4, 1837. He was 34 years old.

It would be pleasing to be able to compare Senator Franklin Pierce's career in the nation's highest legislature with that of the giants of the day: Henry Clay, John C. Calhoun, and Daniel Webster, for example. He served among these men and knew them more or less intimately. But he served almost totally without distinction at a time when distinction was not hard to attain.

First, there was the end of his career as representative. He still served on the Judiciary Committee and, because of his friendship with the party officers in the House, he was chosen to serve on several special committees, including one that attacked the question of the government's banking procedures. But that committee was bogged down in a purely partisan quarrel between Pierce's Democrats and the opposition Whigs and it served no useful purpose. The last week of the session was confusing and tiresome, for the legislators tried to jam through everything they had left undone before March 4, 1837, so they might rush home. With the one session over, the next was called immediately, and Pierce moved to the Upper House to participate in the Inauguration of President Martin Van Buren, to consider Van Buren's appointments to his cabinet and pass on them, and then to go home and wait for winter to arrive once more. While at home, Pierce tried to repair his personal fortunes. For several years, the country had been in a depression, and before this last trip to Washington, Pierce had been forced to borrow $500 to pay off his debts. He put up the house at Hillsborough for sale, but business grew worse and businessmen began to go bankrupt. Pierce considered the problem and blamed it on the United States bank that he and Jackson had opposed so heartily. The bank had tried to keep money so tight that the reaction, when the bank lost power, was for bankers to loosen credit restrictions too much, and the people lost confidence in banks altogether. There were two ways for Pierce to repair his fortune, one by farming and the other through law practice. He worked at both until September, when the situation of the country had grown so severe that the President felt it prudent to call a special session of Congress to deal with the money problems. In the Panic of 1837, the whole country was sorely hurt. The price of commodities fell to the point where farmers let their crops rot rather than sell them at a loss.

When President Van Buren called Congress together, he made certain recommendations. He wanted a new, sound currency based on gold and silver money. (One of the troubles was that state banks were issuing currency based on nothing at all.) He proposed the issuance of $10,000,000 in notes or bonds to cover the government's deficit. (This was the beginning of deficit financing.) He proposed that importers be allowed to pay their customs dues in paper money instead of gold. He proposed the establishment of a new system of subtreasuries in various cities, so the government would keep control of its own money instead of depositing it in various banks as it had been doing.

Senator Pierce listened to the message, read the bills and approved of them all as the best possible measures in this time of crisis. Most of the laws asked for were granted to the new President, although the Whigs won control of most of the state legislatures in the North and the East.

The special session wrecked Pierce's hopes of achieving much financial advancement that year, but he was not displeased, for his protégé Albert Baker could be left to handle the law business, having now passed the bar and secured some experience. In December, Pierce went back to Washington with Jane to attend the regular session. He was one of 52 Senators who debated in the new luxury of the Senate chambers, under a marvelous gilt chandelier. And yet Washington

and the Senate were still rough places; the legislators continued
to live in boardinghouses and drink quantities of whiskey.
(Pierce had quit drinking now.) The streets were still largely
unpaved and threw up such quantities of dust in good weather
that they obscured the view of the passersby. And the Senate
chambers represented the uncouthness of Washington, for the
galleries were directly above the senators on the floor and on
the railing of the gallery was the sign: "You Are Requested Not
to Put Your Feet Through the Railing, as The Dirt Falls on
the Members' Heads."

On the floor, when not being showered with mud or dust,
the senators sat at their desks, bigger and more ornate than
those of the representatives. They wrote with pens on quires
of paper supplied every morning by the pages. The chamber
was heated by four fireplaces, and the senators were always seen
standing before them, spreading their coattails and warming
themselves.

Senator Pierce was a committee worker as he had been when
he was Representative Pierce. That is to say, he did his best
work in committees and seldom made speeches on the floor
that attracted public attention. He was assigned to the Pension
Committee and to the Committee on Manufactures. He
worked in both groups, representing his state but not creating
any stir.

Pierce continued to be strong in his belief that slavery was
a matter for the South and the territories to decide and not for
congressional meddling. His opinion apparently matched that
of his state constituents, for that year Henry Hubbard, the
senior senator from New Hampshire, placed in the hopper
resolutions from the New Hampshire legislature, calling on
Congress to refrain from meddling with slavery. Following
those instructions, Senator Hubbard objected when Senator
Garret Wall of New Jersey offered a petition from his constituents of the Garden State for the elimination of slavery in the

District of Columbia. Just how complicated parliamentary procedure was becoming in this matter was evident.

When Senator Wall offered the resolutions of his constituents, he suggested that they be "tabled," which meant they would be received by Congress and then forgotten. Thus, the right of the people to petition Congress was upheld, but the right of Congress to act as it pleased was also upheld. But Senator Hubbard suggested they shortcut the system that year and that they table Wall's motion. This would mean that the petitions would not be received; all very complicated. Franklin Pierce had recently passed through Boston and knew something of the rising tide of Abolition there. If the Abolitionists could show that Congress would not even accept their petitions, then their cause was being strengthened hour by hour. Pierce objected to this motion, seeing that it would play into the hands of the enemy. So he voted with the Whigs, who were in favor of letting the petitions be heard altogether. Congress still did not act on any of the petitions of the Abolitionists.

Franklin Pierce's senatorial career is more important as a guide to his thinking in later years than for any other reason, for he showed no indications of becoming a leader of the Senate and, in a way, it seemed that he was a most reluctant senator. But as for the issues, they were most revealing, and so were Pierce's reactions to them. The slavery issue had dominated everything else for several years, and now it came to dominate in a way that a cancer spreads, contaminating the tissue around it and eventually enveloping it. That year, the annexation could not be considered without the issue of slavery, for Texas was slave land and would have to come in as a slave state. When the question arose, a senator from Vermont proposed that Texas be refused admission to the Union because she was a slave state.

Thus the fireworks began in the session. Senator John C. Calhoun countered with half a dozen resolutions, determined to protect the rights of the slave states and prohibit congressional interference in the District of Columbia or elsewhere. Franklin Pierce voted *for* these resolutions, and he explained why. Earlier, he said, he had felt that the South was supersensitive on the subject of slavery, and that no great danger to Southern rights or customs existed, except with a lunatic fringe of Abolitionists. But in the past three years, he said, he had seen the Abolition movement grow alarmingly and become the rallying point of many "designing" politicians. Such an alliance of fanatic and politician was very dangerous to the United States, said Pierce and, unless stopped, would eventually lead to a dissolution of the Union.

This revealed the strengthening of Pierce's position against the Abolitionists. With him it was a matter of principle, the principle of states' rights. He was not a slaveowner and did not think like a slaveowner. He considered the question of the rights of the states to be above the rights of human beings. If he is to be faulted in his position, it is for that reason, not because he was without principle. For principle was far more important to men in those days than it would be 100 years later to most politicians. Principle and party loyalty very often went hand in hand as they did in the case of Franklin Pierce. As an uncompromising Jacksonian Democrat, Franklin Pierce had great contempt for the Whigs, who did not even pretend to have a national party but were a coalition of many different groups. Pierce always felt that the Whigs of New England used the slavery issue and the Abolitionists for their own purposes, without any regard for principle.

During that year, an event occurred which was indicative of the strong feeling of the time and Franklin Pierce's entanglement in these affairs. The Pierces were living at Birth's boardinghouse, and one of their special friends was Jonathan Cilley, a representative from Maine, who had been a student at Bowdoin at the time that Pierce was there. Cilley, like Pierce, was a Democrat, and Pierce admired the former's fine flow of invectives on the floor and elsewhere when his old college mate lambasted the Whigs. But one day Cilley implied that a certain Whig editor had taken a bribe in connection with his position on the National Bank, and Kentucky Congressman, William Graves, took issue with him. The matter led to heated words, and a challenge to a duel. Franklin Pierce, along with Thomas Hart Benton, was called upon to help make the arrangements. He and Benton decided on rifles at 80 paces, and one Saturday afternoon the duel was held outside the city. Pierce did not go to the field, but he worried about Cilley's return and, at nightfall, walked out into the dusk to Pennsylvania Avenue to wait for the returning party. A horseman dashed up to him and stopped. Cilley had been killed, he announced.

Pierce whitened, for he was shaken by the news. He was even more shaken in the next few days, when well-meaning editors blamed him for arranging the affair. He wrote a long letter to the newspapers explaining how hard he and others had tried to stop this duel. But the results were unchanged, and the effect on Pierce was to harden him against the Whigs. He believed they had set out to murder Cilley from the beginning because of his strong words and ready tongue and his effectiveness in political battle. The killing also caused Pierce and Jane to reconsider the values of public life and to conclude that they were more interested in returning to rural happiness in New Hampshire than the despicable heat of Washington politics. Indeed, they considered leaving New Hampshire and moving to the West to the pioneer country, to escape the hurly-burly and unhappiness of the times.

"Oh how I wish he was out of political life" Jane Pierce said. And on this note, they went home to New Hampshire that summer.

In the fall of 1838, Franklin Pierce went back to Washington. There were grave matters before the Congress, including much bad feeling with Britain which came about because of American sympathy for a rebellion in Canada and difficulties over the Canadian-American border.

One of Pierce's qualities was a definite independence of spirit and action. He was a Democrat, but he did not subscribe to anyone's policies on such matters as internal improvement. Indeed, even that old curmudgeon, Andrew Jackson, had realized when he was given presidential responsibility, that, in the general interest, the federal government must take certain actions to improve the land of the whole nation. But not Pierce. He stood firm for states' rights and responsibilities. If the Alabama, Florida and Georgia railroad wanted to get going, let the states of Alabama, Georgia and Florida supply the money, not the federal treasury. If some states wanted the Cumberland road, let them put up the money. If there were to be improvements in rivers and harbors, let the various states and cities do their own improvements and not ask the people of New Hampshire to foot part of the bill. New Hampshire wasn't asking for railroad money, or river and harbor money or road money. Let the others mind their own business equally well. As for Texas, he joined the majority who voted to let the matter of annexation wait awhile—a move accomplished by the old process of tabling the legislation.

In preparation for his political retirement, so badly wanted by his wife Jane, Franklin Pierce decided to move from sleepy little Hillsborough to Concord, where there would be much more legal activity and opportunity for financial success. He formed a law partnership with Asa Fowler, who was a student and a "book lawyer," as opposed to Pierce, who was a "talking lawyer." The law business in Hillsborough was left in the hands of Albert Baker. At last, it seemed that he might "make some money." So far Pierce's political activities had barely supported his annual needs, and he had put nothing away.

Pierce's decision to leave politics was partly prompted by the

The law office of Franklin Pierce, Concord, New Hampshire
photo: *The Granger Collection*

fact that in New Hampshire no one was ever reelected to the United States Senate. The stern, hard men of the state did not trust Washington and its influence, even on their own people. So Pierce was a man with nowhere in particular to go in politics. Also, Jane hated Washington, and now, in 1838, she had cause to remain at home; Frank Robert Pierce was born that year. When it came time for Franklin to return to Washington, he went alone.

The Senator's life in Washington was not very interesting. He spent most of his days in committee routine, handling many pension bills for retired and sometimes needy veterans. Thus passed 1838 and 1839, dull years by nearly anyone's standards. Then came 1840 and the rise of the Whig party to seriously challenge the Democrats. Senator Pierce was suddenly very busy again, for he hated Whigs and called them Federalists and Tories as often as he did Whigs. In the state they were to be battled to a standstill. In the nation, he could not abide William Henry Harrison, whose policies Pierce believed to be weak and wrongheaded at best. He could not abide the thought of the country being run by Henry Clay, Daniel Webster and others who represented the old Adams' regime to him. As much as Pierce disliked Van Buren (they had fallen out over a pension matter), he stumped the state for the Democratic President and defended him on 100 stumps. So effective was he that, when the polls were closed in November, Van Buren carried New Hampshire by 6,000 votes—the largest total ever polled in the state. But, of course, New Hampshire was not the Union, and William Henry Harrison was elected President with John Tyler as his Vice–President.

So Franklin Pierce's last two sessions of Congress were spent as a minority party member. The Whigs took control, but then · John Tyler—who was really a Democrat in thought and principle—succeeded Harrison when the latter caught a cold in the Inaugural Parade and died a few weeks later. It was a hectic time—being a minority senator was much more work than being with the majority—and there were Clay and Webster to outfox. But Pierce's heart was not entirely in the battle now; his decision had been made with Jane's concurrence, and on February 16, 1842, he resigned his post as senator and left Washington for Concord, intending to spend the rest of his life as a lawyer dedicated to making money.

5

THE GENERAL
AND THE
MEXICAN WAR

If Franklin Pierce thought he could escape politics by retiring from public office, he was quite wrong. He had gone too far and knew too much about public affairs. His fellows in New Hampshire would not let him sink into the oblivion that Jane would have liked much better than the hurly-burly of public life. True, he held no office in Concord, but he was soon chairman of the state Democratic party and a political power there. In the election of 1843, for example, he spent February and part of March speaking nearly every night in a different town. He joined the reformers and crusaded for temperance. Meanwhile, he suffered a personal tragedy when little Frank Robert Pierce died of typhus fever in the fall of 1843. Pierce's interest in politics was purely local in those days, however, and he did not seek such honors as being elected a delegate to the National Convention. At Baltimore in 1844, James Knox Polk was nominated by the Democrats to oppose Henry Clay, and when the news reached Concord, Franklin Pierce was both surprised and delighted. Polk was his old friend, and Polk stood for everything in the Democratic party that Pierce honored; mostly, he was a moderate on the subject of slavery and was trying to accommodate all parties. Pierce was not philosophically inclined to examine whether all parties could conceivably be accommodated on so vital a national issue. Polk was his man.

Now one of the big questions to New Hampshiremen was Texas: what to do about it? Most of New Hampshire cordially detested slavery and many people were unwilling to bring another slave state into the Union. But Pierce and others pointed out at public meetings that if the United States did not take Texas, Great Britain was almost certain to do so, and that would change the whole situation of the North American continent, and give Europeans—dreaded Europeans—a foothold on our shores.

Pierce was again selected as chairman of the Democratic party in New Hampshire, and this time he promised candidate Polk that the Democrats would carry the state by 6,000 to 10,000 votes. When the party carried New Hampshire by nearly 10,000 votes, Polk was delighted and Pierce's stock was very high with the new administration. He was appointed federal district attorney for New Hampshire, and he continued to lead the party as head of the "Statehouse gang." When John P. Hale, a New Hampshire congressman, decided against supporting the annexation of Texas, Pierce moved swiftly. He nearly had him thrown out of the party and prevented his election as a Democratic congressman. But Hale had his revenge. The temper of the times was changing, and the Whigs allied themselves with certain Democrats, who called themselves Free-Soil Democrats, and broke the party traces over the Texas issue. This alliance sent Hale to the United States Senate in 1846.

That summer, President Polk offered Franklin Pierce the post of United States Attorney General, but Pierce declined. He told the President that he did not want to go back into politics and would not hold public office again, except in time of war. He had many expenses and his family to look after.

But the time of war was fast approaching. The Texas issue was bringing the threat of a war with Mexico, as the United States interfered in the relations between Texas and her old province. War came, and in February, 1847, Franklin Pierce secured an appointment as colonel of infantry in the regular United States Army for the duration of the war, and soon after he was given a commission as brigadier general. He was to raise his own brigade. In May, he left Concord on a fine, black horse, and went to Newport, Rhode Island, and Fort Adams, where his troops were assembling. On May 27, his brigade boarded the bark *Kepler* and sailed for Vera Cruz to augment the army of General Zachary Taylor in Mexico.

Following the declaration of war in May, 1846, Taylor had moved into Mexico and won several victories, but the fighting had bogged down. General Winfield Scott took Vera Cruz in the spring of 1847 and then settled down to reorganize. On June 27, General Pierce and his brigade arrived at Vera Cruz —2,500 men to strengthen the force. Scott had moved on ahead to Puebla and was waiting there for Pierce, before starting the march toward Mexico City.

Vera Cruz, in June, has anything but an enviable climate. Pierce had to get organized before he could march, but he soon saw that the swampland was no place to keep an army even for a few days. To make matters worse nothing was ready. Pierce would have to travel across nearly 100 miles of flat, hot land before there could be any relief at all. Some 2,000 wild mules had been assembled and were supposed to have been trained. But it was all fantasy. The mules stampeded and General Pierce had to wait while they were rounded up and, at least, made tractable enough to pull wagons. Pierce moved his force to the beach, a few miles north of the city, to camp while he waited.

They remained on the beach until July 12, when a shipload

Franklin Pierce as Brigadier General in the Mexican War
photo: The Bettmann Archive

of horses arrived from New Orleans. Then supplies and munitions were loaded into the wagons. Horses and mules were hitched up, and the wagon train set off in sections on July 14. Pierce did not actually get away until the third day. The journey was abominable in the beginning. During the first day's march of five hours, they covered only three miles, because the wagons sank into the sand almost up to the hubs, the mules started and stalled and bowed their necks, and the men gasped in the heat.

The next morning Pierce was up before dawn and had the train on the road. That day, they advanced another five miles. So it went, until the column reached the national highway which stretched from Vera Cruz to the capital and which the government of Mexico had built of concrete. The march changed then. They traveled through the *estancias* of the rich, through the dark rain forest with its bright blossoms, through a wilderness of green filled with strange sounds and animals. They came out onto plains, and then into valleys. They found corn growing and herds of animals. Had it not been for the war, it would have been a beautiful journey, but on June 19, they were attacked by a detachment of Mexicans. The outriders drove off the first force, but at another point of ambush, a Mexican force struck them again. The fighting became brisk before the Mexicans were driven off with several dead and a number of American soldiers wounded.

The next day they marched again, and on the day after, they came to a bridge called the National Bridge. Scouts told Brigadier General Pierce that the enemy had a force posted in the village beyond the bridge, so he was ready for trouble and went out himself to reconnoiter. From the top of a hill above the bridge, the general saw what he would face. Down below was the river, the Antigua, spanned by the bridge; beyond it, on top of a little rise, was the village with a breastwork about 150 feet high above the bridge and looking down on it. There was no way to cross that bridge without falling under the fire of the enemy, unless the enemy was first dispersed. But, there was no way to cross the river and reach the enemy without using the bridge. Brigadier General Pierce decided on a shock assault. The wagons were held back, the troops assembled and they charged across the bridge and up the hill into the breastwork, while the cannon thundered behind to support their action. The breastwork was actually beyond the range of Pierce's guns, but the Mexicans did not know this, and the noise of the guns, plus the charge of the troops, unnerved what must have been raw Mexican troops.

As the Americans began to scale the barricade, the Mexicans broke and ran, the way green troops often do. They had fought gallantly for a few minutes, firing upon the Americans, wounding five and sending a ball through General Pierce's hat. But the thought of a hand-to-hand encounter was too much for them, and in a few moments, the American flag flew above the little fort.

The first camp, other than bivouacks, was at Jalapa, where Pierce was inclined to spend his time in the hotel, until he had a presentiment of danger. The Mexicans he met in the city were just too friendly, he said, and he mounted his horse and rode back to his camp. There he found that one man had already been murdered. They were in the midst of their enemies, and he never again forgot that fact. They moved from Jalapa very soon, commandeering supplies but paying what they considered to be a fair price for them.

Onward and upward they went, climbing to the high plains. With the risk of being ambushed, they headed for the dangerous pass called La Hoya. Toward the end of July, they arrived safely at Perote and, on August 6, reached Puebla. The 2,500 men had marched through 150 miles of enemy country in 21 days, having been attacked six different times by the enemy. It was a considerable accomplishment, but no more than was expected of them. On August 10, an eager Scott was ready to move out toward Mexico City, and they joined the train.

The army of 11,000 moved forward to a point about 20 miles from Mexico City, near Lake Chalco. Scott decided to approach the city from the south, going around Lake Xochimilco. Pierce was working directly under General Gideon Pillow and, on August 18, he was ordered to move forward near San Augustin. There he came up against General Valencia and a large Mexican force. The order was to attack; Pierce from the front, along with General Smith's brigade, while a flanking attack was planned. Pierce mounted his big, black horse and led his men into a field of artillery fire. Luckily the Mexicans were shooting high. He reached a little knoll and stopped there, waving his sword and shouting his men on. A near miss by an artillery shell caused his horse to rear suddenly, then stumble and fall. Pierce was knocked unconscious. An aide reached Pierce, saw he was unconscious and shouted to Colonel Truman Ransom that he must take charge of the brigade. Ransom could not hear, but a loudmouthed officer, named George Morgan, shouted out, "Take command of the brigade, General Pierce is a damned coward."

The "coward" was still unconscious. He had been struck in the groin by the high pommel of his saddle and had wrenched his left knee. His poor horse had broken a leg. In a few minutes, Pierce was struggling toward the scene of action on foot. He was nearly buried by a shell explosion, but he found another horse, got into the saddle and rejoined his brigade. At nine o'clock that night, he was the senior officer on the field and he withdrew the force to a sheltered area. He slept for a few hours, then, sick and bedraggled, he rejoined the brigade in an attack toward General Santa Anna's rear. He appeared before General Scott, who thought Pierce was so sick that he must be sent back, but Pierce refused to go.

"For God's sake, General," he cried, "this is the last great battle, and I must lead my brigade."

Pierce was seeking honor and glory, and there was no doubt about it. How ironic fate could be was shown that day. He led his brigade and leaped one obstacle after another. Then, he twisted his injured knee and fainted from the pain. He fell out of the saddle on the ground, and when his men tried to carry him from the field under fire, he refused to let them. So he lay under fire from the Mexicans for hours, during the Battle of Churubusco. Without his guidance, his men did not behave at all well, and they failed to achieve their objective. Yet Scott was not disappointed in Pierce, and gave him part of the responsibility, along with two other brigadier generals, for arranging the armistice that General Santa Anna now wanted.

The armistice prevented the Americans from sacking the city, but it did not end the war. The peace negotiations failed and, early in September, the fighting began again. General Worth was sent to capture the fortress of Molina del Rey, which was supposed to be a factory for cannonballs. Pierce was put in reserve and came up just at the end of the fighting, again too late to achieve glory. Then came the Battle of Chapultepec —and poor Pierce was flat on his back, with a bad case of dysentery. His second in command and friend, Colonel Ransom, was killed leading the troops that day, and the death might have been Pierce's had his health been good. But as the battle continued, Pierce roused himself—he could stand it no longer—and rode up front, sick as he was. He arrived just as the leader of the assault was preparing the final attack, and he made ready to lead the troops. Just then, a white flag was shown, and the Americans marched into the city without further opposition. Pierce's last chance for glory was gone.

Then came three months of tiresome garrison duty. Pierce's headquarters were in the Calle de Cadena, but he spent much time visiting other headquarters elsewhere in the city. Then on

December 8, General Scott gave a farewell dinner for Pierce and another general, and in a few days they were on their way home. However, Pierce did succeed in earning the goodwill of nearly all the officers and men with whom he had served, because he had remained out of the kind of controversies that divided most of the generals of the Mexican War and had been a friend to everyone he met.

Back he went to Vera Cruz, retracing in peace the route he had followed in war. He went to Washington to report to President Polk. He wanted to resign, but Polk was not sure the war was truly over, so Pierce took a leave of absence. He went to Massachusetts, where Jane was staying with her relatives, and then on to Concord to a hero's welcome. Early next year, the war was definitely over, and the peace treaty was offered to Congress. Pierce came to Washington in February and resigned his commission. He felt certain that he was through with public life in all its forms, and that he had done his duty to family, friends and his country as best he could.

6

THE RELUCTANT CANDIDATE

In the years after the Mexican War, Franklin Pierce became the most important figure in Democratic politics in New Hampshire. He not only kept his party together in the face of much difficulty over Southern problems, he made that party stronger than one might have thought possible. Much of this was accomplished by his own force of character. He was able to accept the views of the South, and while holding to his states' rights concept, he was able to declare with much feeling that the rights of Mississippi must be protected just like the rights of New Hampshire. After so many misfortunes, Pierce and his wife were happy in seeing their son, Benjamin, grow up to be a healthy young boy. Jane Pierce's health improved while she stayed away from the hot and damp climate of Washington. "The General," as he was sometimes called, or "The Dictator," as his enemies termed him blackly, had never been in finer form. His law business prospered. He was, perhaps, the finest trial lawyer in the state, one of those natural orators with a shrewd sense of his audience's reaction and sensitivity to the effect of his words on a jury. He was often called to handle cases for other lawyers. In England, he would have been a barrister instead of a solicitor, for it was on the human side of the law that his talents lay and not in the pages of the musty texts. As biographer Nichols noted wryly, "He didn't convince juries, he converted them." There were civil cases, forgery cases, famous murder cases, slander cases and many damage suits. His most famous cases were known as the "Wentworth murder case" and the "Farnsworth forgery case," and the latter took him as far away from home as Boston.

Meanwhile, as Pierce's life prospered, the Democratic party had fallen on difficult times. In 1848, the Democratic National Convention was turned into an uproarious affair by the injection of the slavery issue as a divisive line between Northern and Southern Democrats. It was not even as simple as that, for there were Northerners who believed in states' rights above all, and who would follow the line. There were others, known as Barnburners, who hated slavery, and among the Barnburners there were two kinds—the Softs and the Hards. The Hunkers, or Hards, were more compromising than the antiadministration Softs, who were firm in their demand that the Wilmot Proviso be the guiding light of the convention. That provision, which had been tacked on to an appropriation bill, had called for prohibition of slavery in American territories. It lost, but it had its effect on American politics.

As can been seen, the slavery issue was beginning to break up the Democratic party, which had held such firm control of much of the nation and the national government for so long. With the exception of the one term of John Quincy Adams, whom Pierce and others described as an unregenerate Federalist, the party—that traced itself to Jefferson—had held office uninterruptedly since 1800. But, in 1848, there were troubles in the Democratic ranks.

Pierce felt himself so far out of things that he did not even attend the Democratic National Convention at Baltimore in

May, 1848. There Polk refused to run again, as he had made clear before, and to compromise, the Democrats chose Lewis Cass of the Western state of Michigan and William Butler of Kentucky. Cass got the nomination for the presidency because he was a man on whom both Northern and Southern men could agree. He was a conservative; the Southerners liked that. He was a Western expansionist; the Northerners liked that. He had backed the principle of "squatter sovereignty," which the Southerners favored. In essence, squatter sovereignty meant that when men and women went to settle on the federal territories, they decided, when the time came—by their votes —whether the territory would be a free state or a slave state. Antislavery Northerners did not like that idea, but the convention got around the objections by nominating Cass, who favored it, and then leaving the matter of squatter sovereignty out of the platform. This was to be the way the party was pasted together in the next few years. The Southerners could not hope to secure adherence to their principles in writing. In other words, the party would have broken up if the Southerners had demanded that everyone subscribe to slavery. But by choosing candidates whom the Southerners knew to be favorable to their cause, and leaving the words unspoken, they kept on going. The platform tried to keep the slavery issue out of the election by declaring that Congress had no right to interfere with slavery in the existing states. The Southerners also wanted a resolution stating that Congress had no right to interfere with slavery in the territories. It was voted down.

The Whigs, stronger now than ever before, chose General Zachary Taylor. He was the ideal American candidate because he was the hero of the Mexican War. Millard Fillmore of New York, a professional politician, was chosen as the vice-presidential candidate. Henry Clay was the leading loser, but Clay had been around too long and was too badly exposed on the tender issues of Texas and slavery. The South still had a very strong influence in both parties, as could be seen by the nominees. Taylor, after all, was a slaveholder on his Louisiana plantation. One cannot overlook the importance of the slavery issue in the nation, in 1848, but it would be wrong to say that it was *the* issue. More properly, the heroism of Zachary Taylor was the issue; the people were conscious of the difficulties of Texas and the territorial problems (should the territories become free or slave states). They knew well the evils of slavery, and they responded, even if negatively, to the old concept of the rights of the peoples of the various states to choose their own way of life. It was, after all, a basic precept of the formation of the Union. They hoped that some good, wise, brave man would arise to lead them out of the political wilderness into which the nation was moving deeper every year. Zachary Taylor gave a strong impression of being just such a man. And that is, primarily, why he was chosen President; he was a proven leader, he was brave and he was someone that everyone liked for his devotion to the Union.

Taylor was elected over Cass and various minority candidates, who represented splinter opinions largely over the issue of slavery. Taylor then set about doing his best. In a divided Congress in which the Free-Soilers—those opposed to extension of slavery—held the balance, President Taylor had a very difficult time. The major domestic issue that came before him first was the question of the admission of California and New Mexico as states. And the problem was made very clear when California applied for admission in 1850. There were 15 free states and 15 slave states in the Union. Californians adopted a constitution prohibiting slavery. The slavery issue was growing hotter.

For eight months in 1850, Congress and the nation immersed themselves in the problem of slavery and politics. That great compromiser, Henry Clay, introduced a series of bills that would have established a formula for settling the differences.

They provided for (1) the admission of California as a free state, (2) no restriction on slavery in the rest of the territory won from Mexico, (3) no interference with slavery in existence in the District of Columbia, (4) no slave trading in the District, (5) strong laws for the return of fugitive slaves, and (6) noninterference by Congress in the slave trade among states.

So the laws were passed, and the "compromise" began. The most important and difficult of these was the Fugitive Slave Law. Many men in the North, who felt that Congress had no right to interfere with the states, would still help an escaped slave rather than send the black man back to his owner. But, the Southerners felt that the test of the truthfulness of the Northerners lay in their willingness to return slaves who escaped. Such sentiments prevailed, while the Abolitionists were strengthening an underground railroad which passed slaves from hand to hand, concealed them from the authorities, and helped them make their way to the Far North, usually to Canada—places from which they could not be brought back.

This Fugitive Slave Law became a central issue in the politics of New Hampshire and a matter of much concern to Franklin Pierce. The Democrats had been very much disheartened by the election of Zachary Taylor on the Whig ticket in 1848, but when Taylor died in office, they began to hope that the Democratic party might pull itself together. Pierce talked much about the lack of unity in the country, and he was distressed by it. But with the election of 1852 coming, he hoped to be able to show that New Hampshire, a Northern state, could live with the attitudes of the South and maintain a union with men of differing cultures. In the autumn of 1850, Pierce stumped the state in behalf of the Compromise of 1850 and fought with vigor for the Fugitive Slave Law as the key legislation involved.

A number of Democrats of the Free-Soil persuasion had secured the nomination of Rev. John Atwood for the governorship of New Hampshire. Pierce approved reluctantly, until he discovered that Atwood had repudiated the Compromise of 1850 and particularly the Fugitive Slave Law. Then Pierce set out to show his power in New Hampshire and the ruthlessness of which any politician must be capable, if he is to hold a high position for long. He secured a meeting of the State Democratic Committee and succeeded in the removal of Atwood as candidate and the election of Samuel Dinsmoor, Jr., as governor. He demonstrated how powerful he was in his home state and that he believed very strongly in the preservation of the Union. He did this for reasons of his own conscience, for he had no personal political ambitions. Indeed, he seldom traveled outside New England these days and looked forward to maintaining his position in local affairs and continuing as the foremost trial lawyer in New Hampshire. He was 46 years old, robust and, like many New Hampshiremen, he regarded politics as a form of intellectual activity and not as a career.

Since the days of John Quincy Adams, no New Englander had achieved the presidency nor, with the exception of Daniel Webster, even the kind of national prominence that makes presidential material. The South was very strongly prejudiced against New England, by and large, because of the influence exerted by the Abolitionists in Boston and in other towns. New York, where there were many people who sympathized with slavery, seemed to be sharply divided from New England in these times.

And yet, in the decade that began in 1850, there was a growing feeling that the nation was in deep trouble, resulting in a constant search by people of goodwill, both in the North and the South, for men who could rise above the issue of slavery and persuade their fellowmen to quiet down. Men above the issue—that is what it was. This was not a surprising development in American politics, because by and large, Americans have voted for men above parties or issues, and the platform has never been as important as the people who carry it. But in the 1850's, it was becoming clear that there was no total escape from the slavery matter because it affected too many people in too many different ways, and the balance of power among the states was not going to work out properly. Had the geography of the United States been different, had the lands of the West been cotton and sugar country, then the slave section of the nation might have hoped to maintain that even split of states. But the West was not slave country, and California's sentiments meant the eventual end of the slave system. The slave states could see the handwriting on the wall. Now they were hoping desperately that places like the Middle West and Far West could be persuaded to adopt slavery, but intelligent men in the South really knew they did not have a chance.

As 1850 rolled along, the Democrats saw the need for a compromise candidate if they were to win the election. There were several such men: Lewis Cass of Michigan, but he was tarnished by defeat; Senator Hannibal Hamlin of Massachusetts; and others who were less well known. Perhaps the leading man was General William Butler of Kentucky, who had run with Cass earlier. But New Englanders did not care for Butler. Then there were James Buchanan of Pennsylvania, Stephen Douglas of Illinois and William Marcy of New York. There was not exactly a dearth of candidates and men who hoped to be candidates, but somehow none of them brought a ground swell of support.

By the beginning of 1852, there was still a good deal of confusion. New Hampshiremen were talking about Levi Woodbury, the old family friend of the Pierces and a staunch Democrat of good standing for a long time, but Woodbury died that year. Franklin Pierce was up to his usual routine of trying law cases and had recently moved into the very lucrative field of corporate law. It paid much better than trying cases for individual clients. Politics was politics, and to advance his own cause for a state office, the Rev. Mr. Atwood was attacking Pierce as a slave sympathizer. Pierce set out to clear the air about that, as a matter of principle, and made many speeches in which he explained his position. He disliked slavery, he said. He disliked the Fugitive Slave Law. But he loved the Union more and was willing to accept what he disliked to prevent the lawmakers from moving along a road that he could see headed straight for a breakup of the United States of America. His arguments were strong. He was popular anyhow, and his views appealed to many who had previously wondered why he sided with the South. State Democrats began talking about Franklin Pierce in new terms, as the "Grand Man" of their state and of New England. They thought he ought to return to national politics and said so at the state convention of the party.

Pierce had many friends elsewhere who believed that he was just the man to unify the Democrats of the North and South. By March, 1852, General Butler's cause was lost. For a short time, it had looked good for him, but he had been available for too long and he made one serious mistake: he endorsed slave-holding in the various territories and did not speak against the Fugitive Slave Law, even in principle, at the right time. This cost him the support of what might be called the moderate Northerners, who cordially disliked the extreme Abolitionists but did not believe in the extension of slavery.

That spring, a group of old Mexican War generals got to-gether in the hope that they could control the nomination of the Democratic party. Chief among them were Caleb Cushing and Gideon Pillow. They schemed all spring and came to Concord to see Pierce. The object was to make sure that if he were nominated he would accept and run for President. How seriously Pierce took their efforts is debatable, but they were old acquaintances as well as men of rank and honor and he certainly did not choose to be rude to them. He was very careful. He insisted that no one use his name unless it became impossible to nominate one of the declared candidates, such as Butler. But enough was known about Pierce's possible candidacy even in May, so that a Richmond editor addressed to him questions he was asking all potential candidates. The questions boiled down to the candidates' answers on the Compromise of 1850. So Pierce answered and, in his answer, gave his basic political position:

. . . If the compromise measures are not to be substantially and firmly maintained, the plain rights secured by the Constitution will be trampled in the dust. What difference can it make to you or me, whether the outrage shall seem to fall on South Carolina or Maine or New Hampshire? Are not the rights of each equally dear to us all? I will never yield to a craven spirit that from consideration of policy would endanger the Union. Entertaining these views, the action of the convention must in my judgment be vital. If we of the North, who had stood by the constitutional rights of the South, are to be abandoned to any time-serving policy, the hopes of democracy and the Union must sink together. As I told you, my name will not be before the convention, but I cannot help feeling that what there is to be done will be important beyond men and parties—transcendentally important to the hopes of democratic progress and civil liberty.

Around June 1, Pierce and his wife went to Boston for a few days and then came back to Concord. Actually, Pierce knew that he was an active candidate, if he could believe his generals. So he waited for the results of the sixth convention of the Democratic party.

This convention met at Baltimore on June 1, 1852. Initially, Franklin Pierce was not mentioned at all—openly. The candidates were Buchanan, Cass, Douglas and Marcy, and on the first ballot Cass led with 116 votes; Buchanan had 93; Marcy,

27; Douglas, 20, and 25 votes were scattered among local favorites. Then came 28 more ballots, with Cass losing strength and Buchanan and Douglas each holding around 90 votes. The convention had adopted the two-thirds rule, which meant that two-thirds of the delegates must vote for a candidate before he could achieve the nomination. By the 29th ballot, many were becoming certain that, at the rate they were moving, they would never agree on a candidate. By the 35th ballot Cass's friends staged a desperate gamble; they put forth all their promises and all their strength and managed to run their candidate's vote up to 131 votes, but that was far short of two-thirds of the 297 delegates.

Pierce had gone to Boston, which was within easy telegraph range of events. He knew he was somewhere in the running, but who knew where? Then Franklin Pierce's name was mentioned, and on the 48th ballot he had 55 votes, and Marcy was leading with 90. But on the floor, the delegates were busy, and the Southerners decided Pierce was a man they could live with. So on the next ballot, South Carolina changed its vote and, within a few minutes, the delegates were standing and shouting to attract the attention of the chair. At the end of the ballot, Pierce had 282 of the votes and was nominated. William R. King of Alabama was selected to be his running mate.

The telegraph brought daily and even hourly word of the progress at the convention, and Pierce was paying strict attention to the news. Yet he was out driving with Jane at the moment when he was nominated. A breathless rider, who galloped up the road after them, found the Pierces between Boston and Cambridge's Mt. Auburn Cemetery. Mrs. Pierce had been dreading the moment, and it seemed so frightful and terrible a prospect to her that she fainted. When she revived, she was most unhappy and brooded for several days as the congratulatory telegrams came into their rooms at the Tremont House. Finally, Pierce took her away from it all to Newport, Rhode Island. However, they did not manage to escape after all, but instead were lionized as Jane had feared.

In accordance with the custom, an official notification committee came to Concord and told Pierce that he was the party nominee. He took them to lunch at the American House and for a steamboat ride on Lake Winnepesaukee. He gave them a formal letter of acceptance, stressing the need for unity and the elimination of "sectional jealousies."

When the Whigs met, they nominated General Winfield Scott for the presidency. The Free-Soil Democrats nominated their own candidate; The Native-Americans, or Know-Nothings, nominated a candidate based largely on his prejudices; the Abolitionists named a candidate on the same basis and so did a Georgia group.

As was the custom, the candidates did very little. General Scott made one campaign trip to the West. The trip was nearly disastrous, because the Whigs found Scott and the party platform to be at odds. Pierce ran a front-porch campaign, writing a few letters, seeing people who came to call and standing on his record. Both major candidates were heartily reviled by their opponents. The old charge of cowardice at the front line was brought against Pierce, and an old court-martial of Scott's was aired again in public. Such evil words were usual in campaigns, and the public took them in the manner it had learned to accept—with a large grain of salt. Pierce did have some problems over which he had little control. New Hampshire excluded Roman Catholics from holding public office, for example, and this infuriated Catholics in other parts of the country, quite understandably. Pierce's position on slavery was also embarrassing.

He had characterized the Fugitive Slave Law as inhumane and morally wrong, but had demanded that it be enforced. Northern Abolitionists and Southern slaveholders both puzzled over that. Pierce contented himself by saying that he had

Presidential campaign poster, 1852
photo: The Granger Collection

been misrepresented and said no more. So the Northern Abolitionists and the Southern slaveholders could guess for themselves which part of the statement was "misrepresentation." Pierce was helped considerably by a campaign biography written by his friend, Nathaniel Hawthorne. It was very useful in the election, but Hawthorne thought so little of it as literature that he never included it in the personal listing of his works.

Then came the election. Pierce carried 27 states and Scott carried Kentucky, Massachusetts, Tennessee and Vermont. Daniel Webster polled 5,000 votes in Georgia, although he had died ten days before the election. The Free-Soilers polled 150,000 votes everywhere, in protest against the national territorial policies.

7

THE
PRESIDENT

Franklin Pierce was a majority President, but just barely. When he was elected and read the returns, he saw how divided the country was between Democrats and Whigs at this time. He had polled 1,600,000 votes, and General Scott had won nearly 1,400,000. That was almost enough to swing the balance if some votes had not gone to other candidates. Pierce's majority, overall, was only 50,000.

Such a situation prompts a new President to look very carefully at the other men and their statements, to see what their appeal had been to the public. Pierce was conscious of a very heavy responsibility, all the more so, because he really had given up public office sometime earlier. He felt the responsibility keenly because he sensed the depth of division between the North and the South over the issue of slavery and states' rights.

Pierce's first task was to form a cabinet that would be indicative of his point of view toward public affairs and give the people an idea of the kind of legislation he proposed to invoke from Congress in the coming four years. One could tell a lot about a man by his cabinet, and the question was whether

Pierce would be the "great ruler" that his friend Nathaniel Hawthorne thought he might become, or the "third-rate" county politician that Richard H. Dana, Jr., said he was. Pierce's approach was to create a "harmony cabinet" which would represent to the people the broadest possible collection of viewpoints. He would heal the wounds of many years within the Democratic party. He would forget past disloyalties from anyone who would accept the Baltimore platform and the Compromise of 1850 as the important law of the land.

Franklin Pierce's triumph was colored by a personal tragedy that winter of 1853. On January 6, as he and Jane and their son Ben were coming to Concord after a trip to Boston, their train was derailed and Ben was killed in the wreckage, although the senior Pierces were scarcely injured. Jane Pierce broke down completely, and Franklin Pierce found it very difficult to keep his mind on the task at hand.

But, finally, he was finished and produced a compromise Cabinet, which he hoped would heal the breaches within the Democratic party and the nation. William L. Marcy and Jefferson Davis would be the symbols of the "unification" at Baltimore. Marcy was a New York Democrat, and Davis was a Mississippian—they represented the reunion of the North and the South in the Compromise of 1850. Marcy would be Secretary of Sate, Davis would be Secretary of War. James Guthrie of Kentucky represented the Middle-South point of view. He would be Secretary of the Treasury. James C. Dobbin of North Carolina would be Secretary of the Navy, another concession to the cotton states. Robert McClelland of Michigan would be Secretary of the Interior, and James Campbell of Pennsylvania would be Postmaster General. Thus, Lewis Cass of Michigan and James Buchanan of Pennsylvania were pacified. Neither would have accepted a place lower than Secretary of State, which Pierce was unwilling to give to either one. Both of them were happy to have been consulted and to have their power

Mrs. Franklin Pierce with her youngest son, Benjamin, 1850
photo: The Granger Collection

acknowledged by the choice of men they had suggested for the positions. Such compromises are the basis for a cabinet chosen by a President. And Caleb Cushing, the Mexican War General, who represented the generals' clique that had brought Pierce to the limelight, was made Attorney General, adding another New Englander. Of all factions within the party, the only one really not represented was that of Senator Stephen A. Douglas, the "Little Giant," who was such an effective champion of Illinois and its people.

So the cabinet was selected, in spite of personal tragedy. Pierce sadly spent the last few days trying to comfort his wife, who was nearly inconsolable. She could not face going to Washington immediately and went to Boston to stay with relatives and friends until after the Inauguration. Pierce left Concord on February 14, and went to Boston to be with her until the 16th, when it was time for him to head for Washington. Personal affairs might pull him, but the affairs of state beckoned and would not wait for triumph or tragedy.

Pierce stopped off in New York and Philadelphia on his way to Washington. It was the practice of all Presidents of the United States, whenever possible, to show themselves in the population centers, because travel was hard in those years, and there were friends and political acquaintances to be seen. In Washington, he stayed at the Willard Hotel. He dined with President Fillmore at the White House. He worked on his Inaugural Address. He went to inspect a new ship at the Alexandria docks. He received delegations, one of which gave him a horse and carriage. He was busy, although personally very sad and subdued, until Jane Pierce arrived in Baltimore on March 1, where she would stay for a time. He went to see her and then returned to duty.

On March 4, President-elect Franklin Pierce rode with President Fillmore to the Capitol for the Inaugural ceremony. Vice President-elect King was sick in Cuba, so there was no ceremony for him, as there usually was for the second-in-command of the State. In the Senate Chamber, before the Congress, the Supreme Court and the diplomatic corps, President Franklin Pierce took the oath of office from Chief Justice Taney and became the 14th President of the United States. He spoke bravely in his Inaugural Address in favor of national expansion, for peace, for trade expansion, for economy in government, and then he came to the matters that were gripping the nation by the throat in 1853.

He spoke first of his love for the Union—"my best and dearest earthly hopes are entwined . . ."

Then he spoke about slavery. "I believe," he said, "that involuntary servitude, as it exists in different states of this Confederacy, is recognized by the Constitution. I believe that it stands like any other admitted right, and that the states where it exists are entitled to efficient remedies to enforce the constitutional provisions. I hold that the laws of 1850, commonly called the 'Compromise Measures' are strictly constitutional and to be unhesitatingly carried into effect."

He said he hoped the question of slavery had been put to rest by the Compromise of 1850, and that no further issue would be made of it.

"We have been carried in safety through a perilous crisis," he added. "Wise counsels, like those which gave us the Constitution, prevailed to uphold it. Let the period be remembered as an admonition, and not as an encouragement, in any section of the Union, to make experiments where experiments are fraught with such fearful hazard."

So it was over. If Pierce believed, truly, that the issue of slavery had been set at rest by the Compromise and his firm announcement that he would adhere to it, then he was fooling himself, and he did not give such indication in his careful selection of the cabinet. For the moment, he must go back and take the plaudits of the many at the Inaugural Reception,

The Inauguration of Franklin Pierce, 1853
photo: *The Granger Collection*

which was traditional at the White House since Jackson's day. There was to be no Inaugural Ball because of the tragedy in the Pierce family, but there was a reception and he shook a thousand hands that afternoon. It was late in the evening, before he finally found a bit of peace and a bed in the confused and disordered apartments of the President.

The new administration began in earnest the next day, when Pierce settled in at the White House. He found the three rooms in the southeast portion that were set aside for official business, and took over the big desk of Andrew Jackson in the room that also served as a cabinet room. Then he moved his belongings to the other side of the second floor, where the family apartment would be located, to be arranged by Jane as soon as she found the strength to face the new life. Pierce had a few problems that kept him from worrying too much about his new estate. One was that although he had selected Jefferson Davis for the cabinet, Davis had not yet accepted. Over this weekend, before Congress assembled to act on the presidential appointments, Pierce had to make sure he had a Secretary of War. Davis came to call; Pierce used his most convincing tones, and the Mississippian gave up his hopes of life on the pleasant plantation and undertook the job.

Socially, the Pierce administration was anything but a success. Pierce was almost alone in his meetings with the public. Jane Pierce let others run the White House, and let herself sink into so total a depression that she spent most of the time sitting alone in her room, thinking about her lost son, and even writing him tender little letters. And Pierce changed too, as Presidents will change from the men they were before. He had given up drinking many years ago. He could still be the gay conversationalist of the old days, but there was a more sober mood upon him usually, as he contemplated the problems of a nation that was badly split over a basic issue that threatened to tear it apart.

Pierce's first task was to present his cabinet to the Congress.

Jane Pierce's Inauguration dress

After this was done and the cabinet was accepted, he had to meet with these seven men daily and make some 700 appointments to office as quickly as possible. Here he came up against the nation's growing factionalism, which meant that every appointment had to be considered geographically and in the light of the applicant's views on slavery, in addition to everything else. There was only one way to approach the matter, in Pierce's mind, and that was to forget all about the past and make the appointments on the basis of the man's willingness to abide by presidential policy. Even a Whig was retained— John Wilson—in the land office, because he was so good at his job. And Pierce made one interesting departure from precedent: he chose an appointee to fill a vacancy on the Supreme Court who was recommended by the justices themselves. The new appointee was John A. Campbell of Alabama, and he was accepted by all the justices, whether Whig or Democrat. Certainly, Pierce began his administration with an eye toward pleasing the nation and quieting down the most difficult situation ever faced in America. In the rest of his patronage, he relied finally on the cabinet officer who controlled the jobs, and he managed to make the others accept appointments in their states that they might not otherwise have countenanced.

Among the appointments, one was to Nathaniel Hawthorne as consul at Liverpool, which Pierce made to reward his friend and biographer. Hawthorne accepted it in the hope that he would make enough from the consular fees for a few years to become independent and never again have to write anything he did not care to write. Another was that of James Buchanan as minister to England, an appointment that helped Buchanan's career and made him a strong candidate for the next election. As it turned out, the sojourn in England kept Buchanan out of political trouble on the slavery issue at a time when it was at its peak.

By Independence Day, President Pierce had finished the

troublesome patronage task and could turn to other matters. Among the difficulties were those in foreign affairs, and chief among those problems were issues involving Great Britain, Mexico and Spain. As far as Britain was concerned, the Clayton-Bulwer Treaty of 1850 had not settled all the issues between the United States and England, although it did stop America from building its own canal across Panama. But part of the agreement was that the British would stop extending their financial interests in Latin America, and now there were disquieting reports that Britain was not living up to this commitment. Furthermore, there was difficulty about fishing rights off the Canadian coast.

Concerning Mexico, the treaty that ended the war had been less than definite about certain boundaries, particularly the isthmus of Tehuantepec and the Mesilla Valley. And certain American-based adventurers, known as filibusters, were using the resources of the United States to plan expeditions to Mexico, whereby they hoped to set up independent little kingdoms. In these days of confusion in Latin America, it was much the rage for adventurers to think they could get rich and establish their own dukedoms in the South, and "filibustering" excited many a young man as "privateering" had excited them in days past. The difference was that privateering, at least, pretended to be in the interest of the mother country against her enemies, while filibustering was nothing more than organized piracy.

Spain was not very happy with the United States over the question of Cuba. Earlier administrations had tried to acquire Cuba, and had offered as much as $100,000,000 for the island, but the Spanish government was not interested in selling. Since that time, the filibusters had been attacking Cuba or threatening to attack, quite regularly, and the Spanish were much aroused.

Then there was a new policy, a part of Manifest Destiny, or the expansion of the United States to the west. When the

West Coast of the American continent was reached, and the United States became a huge power in terms of geography, suddenly Hawaii, the Pacific Islands and the Asiatic Mainland became of great interest to Americans. Commodore Matthew Perry had been sent off under a previous administration to establish trade relations with Japan. Pierce and his Secretary of State, William Marcy, considered the opening of China a matter of grave interest to the United States as well, and Robert McLane was sent there for the purpose of seeking reciprocal free trade from the Chinese Empire—and to use Perry's fleet to force an agreement, if that became necessary.

And finally, the Pierce administration was to make one very popular move in the matter of American prestige and foreign affairs that first summer of 1853; it was called the Koszta affair.

Martin Koszta was a native of the Austro-Hungarian Empire, who came to the United States and became a citizen. But, in 1848, he went back to Smyrna, in the Empire, and was so emotionally involved with the old country that he engaged in certain revolutionary activities there. He was arrested in the summer of 1853 and held aboard an Austrian warship, which was going to make sure that he went to Vienna for a trial. Captain Duncan Ingraham of the United States Navy happened to be in Smyrna at the time, with his warship the *St. Louis*. Captain Ingraham took the arrest as an insult to the American flag, when Koszta claimed protection of the United States. He said he would fire on the Austrian ship unless Koszta was turned over to him. The Austrians turned Koszta over to the French consul to stop the affair, and then the Austrian government protested in Washington against Captain Ingraham's action. "An outrage," they called it.

Pierce and Secretary Marcy studied the evidence and then wrote a letter to the Austrians denying their claims. In September, the interchange of letters was released to the public and brought much acclaim to President Pierce and his administration.

It was a sign of the times, however, that his appointments aroused much antagonism. Probably nothing Pierce could have done differently would have helped because the nation was dividing. The criticism from outside was that he appointed men from every walk of life. The criticism from within the Democratic party—which brought new ammunition to the Whigs—was that he appointed "radicals" like Jefferson Davis as well as Abolitionists. They were, at the very least, men who had favored the Wilmot Proviso. He was criticized for not appointing Democrats who had supported the Compromise of 1850.

Pierce's reason, of course, was to try to heal the wounds of the past, but now the wounds would not heal, and this became apparent very early in the game. Whatever he might have done, there was too much excitement about slavery. The dangers to both sides seemed too near and too apparent and the Administration could not have pleased the activists. Clay, Webster and Calhoun were all gone; and no matter what else might have been said of this triumvirate, they *had* controlled the Congress for nearly 40 years, bending it to their wills. And, although they were three individuals—not even friends—they knew and understood one another. While they were alive and working, there was chance for compromise. But to replace them, there were no great figures of equal stature, no men of courage and conviction who could carry the battles of the sections in their own inimitable ways.

Instead, the nation seemed to be afflicted with many petty men.

Pierce was beset almost immediately with a bad or unfriendly press. Here is the way it worked, in one instance. C. Edwards Lester of New York had hoped to be appointed to high office by President Pierce. He was disappointed and, in the manner of many office seekers, he did not take the disappointment lightly. At the time, he held a post as correspondent for the London *Times*, and he used that position to assault the administration. Elsewhere, disappointed Democrats started grumbling. The trouble was, of course, that the Democratic party was frightfully fragmented. There were the Cass supporters of the West—and the Cass enemies. There were the Hards and the Softs of the Barnburners of New York, and the anti-Barnburners of New York. There were the hard-shell union men, who objected to appointments of Southerners. There were Southern extremists who objected to nearly everything. And because the party was so fragmented, every disappointed office seeker found friendly ears into which he might pour his tale, and then he went about redoubling his noise. The press hurt the most. There was nothing so venal, it seemed, as a writer scorned. Francis J. Grund, a correspondent for the Philadelphia *Public Ledger* and the Baltimore *Sun*, wanted a consulate. He did not get it, and immediately he began attacking the administration and all its works. It was a typical performance. Pierce might have ignored all of it and gone ahead with his work, but he made what might have been a most serious mistake when he decided to pay attention to the gibes and establish his own press. He got friends to take over the *Union* of Washington and turned it into the administrative organ, thus further annoying other newspaper editors, who saw evil in every friendly article in the *Union*.

Pierce decided to make a trip to the North for public-relations purposes. He went to Philadelphia and saw Buchanan as well as many other Democratic leaders. The train stopped at Trenton, Princeton, New Brunswick, Rahway and Elizabeth. It finally came to the end of the line at Newark. The next day, he went to New York and appeared at Castle Garden to celebrate the United States World's Fair. He made a long, but not very successful, speech and presented a rather bedraggled appearance which did not work in his favor. He drank some brandy, perhaps more than was good for him, and the point was noticed by his party.

During this first year, the Democrats won the initial set of off-year elections, most of them in the South, and Pierce began to feel victorious. But in the summer, the Whigs showed new strength in elections in Alabama and North Carolina, and this was worrisome. And then again, more bitterness arose about appointments—which could not have happened had there been real party discipline among the Democrats.

Pierce appointed John Y. Mason as Minister to France, and this infuriated James Gordon Bennett, the New York *Herald* editor who wanted the job. The *Herald* turned against Pierce, joining the *Post* and the *Tribune*. Poor Pierce could do no right in New York. By the end of the year, the rebellion had spread across the nation, into the North, and even into New Hampshire, where his old friends were now saying that Pierce was soft with their enemies. Everybody, it seemed, was saying the same thing. Without having either succeeded or failed Franklin Pierce had lost the confidence of his own party. Or, one might say, the party had lost confidence in itself and in its abilities to hold together.

Then, also, Pierce approached the most serious of all his problems—the relationship of the various sections of the country which threatened to tear the nation apart. He spoke to Congress of the future, a future where, in 1900, he saw the nation numbering 100,000,000 people. (He was right.) He warned that such a large nation could succeed only if the principle of states' rights was firmly guarded, and he spoke again of "forebearance, respect, and noninterference." It read very well and it sounded very pleasant. In spite of an unfavorable press, which could largely be laid to bad temper on the part of a few, Pierce's initial months here indicated a breathing spell perhaps, when the nation might bind up its sores and hope for better times. He, in particular, saw in the movement toward the West, in the expansion of trade and business and in American hopes the way out of the dilemma. If there was enough of everything, then perhaps men would be able to rise above the sectionalism that had been troubling the country so sorely for the last few years.

It was a marvelous hope.

8

KANSAS AND NEBRASKA I

The 33rd Congress, which was called together in December, 1853, gave President Pierce a comfortable majority of Democrats in the House as well as in the Senate, so one might have expected him to have an easy time of it. But the fact was that by 1853 the Democratic party was so fragmented as to be scarcely a political party at all. Only with utmost difficulty could the administration retain "party regularity," and Pierce was not always capable of managing that, as events showed.

The Congress was looking for leadership. With the death of the triumvirate, Pierce turned to Senator Charles G. Atherton of his native New Hampshire, but Atherton died and left a serious vacuum. Into it, slowly stepped the "Little Giant," Senator Stephen A. Douglas, who had absolutely no responsibility to the administration personally because he had been ignored in the patronage lottery. This fact was to become one of the burdens of Pierce's administration.

In the beginning of 1854, public and congressional agitation were strongly in favor of the opening of more of the Western territories to settlement and inclusion in the Union. Pierce was not particularly pleased with this state of affairs. Like many other rulers, the President recognized the dangers of his internal political situation, and he proposed to take the people's minds off their differences by excursions into foreign expansionism and a vigorous policy of fighting waste and dishonesty in the government. Foreign expansion was to include the purchase of Cuba, the extension of American trade into Latin America and across the Pacific, and the tidying up of the American-Mexican border situation. Domestic policy was to clean up graft, assertedly left over from the four years of Whig management. In all this, Pierce hoped very definitely to hide the unsolved problem of states' rights versus human rights or slavery. Bravely, he often told himself and those around him that the Compromise of 1850 had permanently resolved the question of slavery in the states. Working against Pierce's good-will were the prime movers of "Manifest Destiny," the expansion philosophy.

With the coming of fall and a legislative program to be presented to Congress, Franklin Pierce had a chance to undo the evil that his selfish friends and acquaintances were heaping on him because he didn't do their bidding. When President Pierce made his annual State of the Union Address to Congress, he showed his own limitations—the most important of these was his unwillingness to experiment. This included his insistence that the spirit and letter of the Constitution be maintained, that the Founding Fathers had created the perfect instrument, and that no one could better it or ought to try. Here was his great weakness as a statesman.

Pierce and his cabinet faced a problem that bedeviled several Presidents in the early days of the Republic: a surplus in the treasury that threatened to eat up all the cash in the land and keep it in the government's vaults. It seems a joke in the 20th century that a surplus would cause trouble, but it very definitely did so, and Pierce and Treasury Secretary Guthrie made plans to reduce the amount. It kept coming in through the sales of public lands, but by revising tariffs downward—and not collecting so much money—the surplus could be controlled. This was one of Pierce's plans for the future. The army and navy secretaries wanted to increase their forces and equipment, and Pierce advocated this, too, as a means of cutting the treasury surplus. He also approved land grants for the railroads and a reorganization program for the federal courts, which were falling behind in their work because of the growth of the nation. There had been talk about a railroad to the Pacific, and Pierce approved of the idea, but he did not believe that government should play any role other than as encourager. He was a firm believer in private business enterprise. The American move westward had bulged up now against the frontiers of the unorganized territory. That does not mean to say that people were not already in the territory; they were, but the niceties and protections of lawful civilization were not. The railroad men wanted to go in, they wanted land grants and they wanted protection. Already Congress had provided for surveys and preliminary work that indicated the railroads would be moving west. One of the first moves, the breaking of the treaties and the seizure of the lands from the Indians, was well under way, led by the gentle guidance of George W. Manypenny, head of the Office of Indian Affairs who was in Kansas, laying waste to the Indian rights.

In December, 1853, when Congress met, members of both Houses came armed with bills to organize the Nebraska Territory. Senator Douglas was one of these, and he was not entirely free from a personal interest in railroad and land speculation. On January 4, 1854, he introduced a bill in the Senate to organize the Nebraska Territory. But he soon ran against Southern opposition. Senator David Atchison of Missouri brought the matter to a head: the bill must somehow resolve completely the question of the Missouri Compromise of 1820, which had forbidden slavery in the northwestern part of the Louisiana Purchase. The Southerners said that the Compromise of 1850 had indicated the way, but they did not feel it was strong enough to do the job properly. They disagreed with Pierce that the issue was settled, and they insisted that the issue be resolved by leaving up to the people of the territories involved the manner in which they should live, with or without slavery.

When Atchison made his position clear to Douglas, the Illinois Senator realized that he had to go along with the South, or there could be no expansion west. To understand this feeling and all that happened in Pierce's administration, one must have an understanding of the makeup of the Congress— particularly of the Senate—that existed in this period. In the House of Representatives, there were 158 Democrats and 72 Whigs. The strongest was the Virginia delegation, which boasted the chairmenships of the Committee on Foreign Affairs and the Committee on Naval Affairs. An Alabaman, named George Houston, was chairman of the Ways and Means Committee. There were many Democrats from Pennsylvania and New York, and they were often divided among themselves on the slavery issue. The Democracy, as it called itself then, was very strong in the West, and the House members were quite responsive to Senator Douglas. Of 16 major committees, the Southern states held control of six, counting Whigs and Democrats—which one *must* do on sectional issues —and the East controlled only two committees, Manufactures and Pensions. The South, even then, had a long list of members with seniority, as opposed to the East and West.

The Senate was indicative of Pierce's problem and the state of the Union at that time. The most prominent senator was Lewis Cass of Michigan, but "Old Cass" was in his dotage and regarded more as a windbag than as a force in the Senate. "Judge" Douglas was the real leader, and even though he had failed to achieve the presidential nomination in 1852, it was generally accepted that he was the man to look to for the future. The Southerners feared and distrusted him. There were several other Western senators, who owed most of their loyalty to Douglas and Western expansion.

Four men represented the interests of the South and dominated all the other Southerners. They were Atchison of Missouri, who was Acting Vice–President after the death in Cuba of Vice–President King, and thus the next in line of succession in case Pierce should die. James Mason of Virginia was chairman of the Senate Foreign Relations Committee and a real power. Andrew P. Butler was chairman of the Judiciary Committee, and this South Carolinian was very powerful, too. Finally, came Robert Mercer Taliaferro Hunter of Virginia, the last of the four, and chairman of the Finance Committee. Together with their allies, the four could block nearly any legislation. Another powerful Southerner, and an enemy of Pierce because he wanted to be a cabinet secretary or a minister and did not get a post, was John Slidell, once of New York, and now of Louisiana. Another was Sam Houston of Texas.

There were 37 Democrats, 22 Whigs and two Free-Soil men. Twenty-one of the Democrats were from the free states, but the South held those three important committees, and Western senators held eight of the major chairmanships, while the Easterners had but five. Obviously a combination of the West and the South could rule, so when Atchison came to Douglas and told him what must be done, Douglas listened attentively.

What Atchison wanted was an outright "repeal" of the Missouri Compromise and its restrictions on slavery in the territories. Douglas knew that the Abolitionists would put up a fearful howl if this were attempted, and he convinced Atchison, on the surface anyhow, that the best course was to take an indirect route. He went back and redrew his territorial law

to organize the territories of Kansas and Nebraska, divided at
the 40th parallel. He used the same phrases that had been used
in organizing the territories of Utah and New Mexico, which
said the territorial legislatures had all powers of legislation
consistent with the Constitution. Slavery was not excepted.
The question of the presence of slaves in the territories was to
be decided by the courts, and Utah and New Mexico, under
the law, should be received into the Union "with or without
slavery," depending on what the people of the new states
wanted at the time of their admission. Thus, in making up his
bill, Senator Douglas ignored the Missouri Compromise, and
practically outlawed it, if the Kansas-Nebraska Bill should pass.
In the report that accompanied the measure in Congress,
Douglas and his committee said that they did not consider the
Missouri Compromise, but addressed themselves totally to the
later Compromise of 1850 in their considerations, particularly
the point that "all questions pertaining to slavery in the territories and new states to be formed therefrom, are to be left to
the decision of the people residing therein, through their ap-
propriate representatives."

All might have been well, had not a Southern Whig, named
Archibald Dixon, decided to play politics with the bill and
show how much more wedded to the South were the Southern
Whigs than the Democrats. He attached an amendment to the
bill which specifically outlawed the old Missouri Compromise
and its antislavery provision. Then, the Southern Democrats
had to accept that provision in order to stay popular at home.
And to top off matters, Senator Charles Sumner, a Massachusetts man, added another amendment, to reenact the Missouri
Compromise restriction on slavery. So the slavery issue heated
up again.

Pierce and his cabinet tried to smooth matters over by offer-
ing an amendment that would limit the rights of persons and
property to the restrictions of the Constitution and the courts.

Franklin Pierce sitting on the shoulders of Lynn Boyd, Speaker of the House, with Stephen A. Douglas, holding the Nebraska Bill on the left, and Senator Thomas Benton on the right.

photo: The Bettmann Archive

This was taken to the Southerners, who refused it and demanded the repeal of the Missouri Compromise. Douglas went to see Pierce over the weekend, because he had to have his bill ready by Monday, and it had to be right. He took Jefferson Davis with him. Pierce saw them. He had pledged that he would never reopen the slavery controversy, which he said was settled by the Compromise Measures of 1850, yet here he was in apparent conflict with the Senate, which must accept his appointees and ratify his treaties. So Pierce made a statement that "the Missouri Compromise was superseded by the principles of the legislation of 1850, commonly called the Compromise Measures, and is hereby declared inoperative and void. . . ." The people of the territories, he said, were to be able to form their domestic institutions, such as slavery, in their own way.

The next day the amended bill was presented to Congress. Pierce had made his great and fatal error. He had promised himself and others that he would not become involved in the slavery issue, and yet here was the first major foray of his administration, and he was deeply committed. On January 24, 1854, Senator Sumner and Senator Salmon P. Chase and others who believed in the Missouri Compromise put forth an "Appeal of the Independent Democrats" which called the new measure a "gross violation of a sacred pledge" and charged that Pierce had become the creature of the Southerners. The debate began.

The New York *Tribune* lost no time in attacking Pierce, and Abolitionist journals followed very quickly. For three months, the Senate debated the measure, and the newspapers reported the debates, and public heat spread. Pierce saw that he was in trouble, but he could not back down on his own statements. What he must do, he saw, was bring the Northern Democrats around to support the measure as a party doctrine. He put his pressure on Senator Hannibal Hamlin of Maine, but Hamlin did not respond. Still, when the votes were counted, the measure passed by 37 votes for and 14 against. To Pierce's satisfaction, among the 37 were 14 Northern Democrats. The bill passed the Senate on March 3, but getting it through the House of Representatives was another matter. What happened to the Kansas-Nebraska measure was that it got thoroughly involved in political "logrolling," or the exchange of support by a member of the House for one measure he did not care about if someone else would support a measure he did care about. Involved at this time was a Homestead Bill, which liberalized the laws granting homesteads to settlers, and a bill providing for the location of two Pacific railroads, one through the present state of Nebraska, and one through Kansas. Also, there was a rivers and harbors bill, which always involved logrolling by those who would benefit from federal support of harbor improvement (such as the port cities), and a bill providing for the erection of public buildings in certain areas, which meant more logrolling. Thus, the Kansas-Nebraska Bill in the House became a matter of lining up blocs who wanted this bill or that one and making trades. It was much less a matter of Democratic and Whig politics than of regional politics, and practically not at all a matter of political principle.

Meanwhile, as the House debated and traded, in Massachusetts the Emigrant Aid Society was formed. The purpose of this society was the promotion of antislavery sentiment in Kansas, so that when the territory became a state, the antislavers would outnumber the slavers. And to match this—even before the law was passed—various secret groups in the South began promoting the movement of slaveholders with their slaves into Kansas, so that when the time came, the state would be slave. The pressure was building and building.

All spring, President Pierce and his cabinet fretted. Late March brought a motion to commit the bill in the House to the Committee of the Whole, which might have killed it. Pierce remained confident that it would pass, and that then there would be no more trouble about the territories. One of his basic reasons was that he knew—and so did everyone else —that neither the land nor the potential agriculture on the land would lend themselves to slave labor. There would be no cotton or sugarcane to grow in Kansas, and the wheat, the cattle and the small crops did not require slaves; in fact, did not make slave labor even theoretically practicable. Southern friends agreed, but insisted that while all these Northern lands *were* useless for slaveholders as agricultural lands, there was the matter of principle involved.

The proponents and opponents struggled nearly all spring. In the end, President Pierce and his partisans were victorious, and the bill passed, although only by 113 votes to 100, with party lines destroyed time and again, and 21 House members choosing to be absent rather than be involved at all. (The party strength of the Democrats was 158.) On May 30, both Houses had passed the bill, and President Pierce signed it into law with a sense of grave relief. Here at last, he was certain, he had settled the question of slavery agitation once and for all.

9

THE EXPANSIONIST

President Franklin Pierce was dedicated to the growth and strengthening of the United States as a world power, and his vision of a big country taking its place in world affairs was far beyond that of most of the men around him. Given a united America, he might have become one of the great Presidents, for his sense for foreign affairs was much surer than his domestic sense.

In May, Pierce, at the suggestion of Jefferson Davis, had sent James Gadsden of South Carolina to Mexico as a minister. Gadsden's major task was to negotiate a settlement of a boundary dispute that arose from the Treaty of Guadalupe Hidalgo at the end of the Mexican War. Gadsden negotiated and signed a treaty under which Mexico received $15,000,000 for which she gave the United States a strip of territory totaling about 30,000 square miles in the Mesilla Valley south of the Gila River—in what is now Arizona and New Mexico. Pierce was vastly disappointed, because the amount of land was so small and because certain territorial claims were not all settled. For a month he worried about the matter, and then, in February, he sent the treaty to the Senate. There was something else to worry about while the Kansas-Nebraska Bill was under debate. There was his reason for letting Douglas have his way, so the President could have his treaty. Pierce considered territorial expansion and his conduct of foreign relations to be far more important than the Kansas-Nebraska problem.

A foundation stone in Pierce's foreign policy was the firm belief that France and Britain were in league to harm American interests. He might have been closer to the truth if he thought that France and Britain did not care a fig for American interests, where those interests conflicted with their own, as in Latin America. But Pierce had a grand idea of the American dream, and he must be forgiven for thinking in terms of the future and not in terms of the problems of his own day. His associates also strengthened his fears of Britain.

One of the first issues to be faced in the spring of 1854 was the Spanish seizure of the cargo of the American steamer, *Black Warrior*, in Cuba. The Spanish claimed that the ship had violated Cuban port rules. When the word came in March, the newspapers and public arose in fury. They demanded no less than the dispatch of warships to Havana. Congress began to debate the matter, and Secretary Marcy prepared a demand for an apology from Spain for no fewer than 16 cases of Spanish disregard for American rights in Cuba. Just about this time, Marcy learned of a possibility that Cuba would be for sale and instructed the American minister to begin negotiations. And then, in April, Marcy and Pierce set in motion plans to purchase Alaska from the Russians and to annex Hawaii. Here was a very vigorous foreign policy, indeed.

The Mexican Treaty was ratified in June (for a payment of $10,000,000 instead of $15,000,000). By this time, Cuba was proving to be a headache. The filibusters, noting Pierce's attitude and interest, began concentrating their activities in the area. Senator Slidell suggested that the neutrality laws of the

United States be suspended, which would allow the filibusters to do as they please. General John Quitman, a noted filibuster, announced the organization of an expedition in New Orleans to free Cuba from the Spanish—and bring it under Quitman. The Southerners were very frightened, lest the Spanish government free the Cuban Negroes and create a new problem for them just a few miles across the water. Such a move was definitely reported by secret American agents in Cuba.

Pierce and Secretary Marcy could scarcely negotiate with Spain for Cuba if they let filibusters overrun the island, so Pierce stopped Quitman's Cuban expedition. But the negotiations broke down.

Pierce was still beset with the Kansas-Nebraska issue, when an old dispute with the British and Canadians was finally settled very favorably by a Reciprocity Treaty negotiated between Secretary Marcy and Britain's Lord Elgin, Governor General of Canada. The United States won fishing privileges along the inlets of New Brunswick, Nova Scotia, Quebec and Prince Edward Island. The British could then fish legally down to the 36th U.S. parallel. Pierce was delighted. He looked upon the treaty as the first in a line of changes that would eventually bring about a merger of the United States and Canada and the creation of an even greater power on the North American continent.

Latin American problems continued, one of them brought about by Commodore Cornelius Vanderbilt's own expansionism. The Commodore had been as responsible for the Clayton-Bulwer Treaty as anyone, for he had once proposed to build his own canal across Nicaragua, and that had put the wind up with the British during the Polk administration. All this, of course, stemmed from the days of the California gold rush, which had caused various American firms to establish steamship lines down the East Coast of the U.S. to Panama and Nicaragua. These firms then ran stages and trains across the steamy isthmus land, and finally steamer lines were established from Panama and Nicaragua up to San Francisco. Vanderbilt's Accessory Transit Company was constantly in hot water with the authorities at Greytown, in Nicaragua, which was really a British dependency, under the guise of a "protectorate" over the Mosquito Indians. At about this time, unpleasant affairs broke out when a captain of Vanderbilt's was arrested for murder, and the American minister to Nicaragua interfered personally in the case. Americans at home shouted that the government had to protect Vanderbilt and American interests. The issue steamed in the hot Nicaraguan sun.

The real trouble with the Cuban problem was that Congress would not give the administration money to buy the island.

August Belmont, the banker, who was the agent of the Rothschild family in Europe, suggested that the executive branch could make arrangements through private bankers in Europe to buy the island if it became necessary, and so Pierce continued his negotiations. But he was so unwise as to tell too many people what he was doing, and the word got around Europe, which made it impossible for the Spanish government to negotiate seriously without seeming to show weakness. The Cuban annexation, then, came to nothing, and whatever hopes were revived from time to time, they still amounted to nothing.

Nicaragua became a troublesome focal point and a center of bad American-British relations, but Cuba always remained the hope of Pierce. Pierre Soulé, the American minister to Spain, was the one who fumbled the job. Soulé was a Louisiana politician who thought he could carry out the Spanish mission. He had begun by demanding very rough treatment at the time of the *Black Warrior* incident. In the summer of 1864, he met with John Mason, the minister to France, and James Buchanan, the minister to Britain. In the fall, on the basis of that meeting, the ministers made a declaration which was later called the Ostend Manifesto. It declared that Cuba was vital to American interests, especially the security of slavery. The fact was that Cuba was undergoing revolutionary torments and the revolutionaries threatened that one of their first acts, when successful, would be to free the slaves of Cuba—which would bring thunder on the heads of American slaveowners. The American ministers' language was very intemperate. They indicated that if the United States could not buy Cuba we should seize it, and when the paper was published months later, it brought much criticism against Pierce from every quarter, both in the United States and in foreign countries.

The Nicaraguan problem was exacerbated by generally bad relations between the United States and Britain. During the Crimean War, the United States insisted that American cargoes be left undisturbed no matter to whom they were bound or in whose ships they were carried. British policy stiffened in Central America, and Commodore Vanderbilt and his friends tried to make capital of the weak Nicaraguan government for their own ends. Pierce complained that both Britain and France violated the Monroe Doctrine constantly, and that they kept us from obtaining a coaling station for our navy at Santo Domingo by interfering with the government of the Dominican Republic. We wanted Samaná Bay, but the British and French raised so much fuss that the Dominican government backed out. In 1855, a Colonel Henry L. Kinney acquired a grant of land near Greytown, and announced his intention of building an agricultural settlement there and attracting Americans. Since Kinney had been entertained at the White House, this was regarded by the British as an American expansion plan, which it was. More fireworks followed. Wherever President Pierce turned in his quest for expansion, he seemed to meet either with outright interference from the European powers, or with negative attitudes from Congress.

The tragedy of it was that the negativism in Congress arose from a domestic problem, the overwhelming problem of Kansas and Nebraska, which that year became the symbol of the slavery issue in the United States. It was increased by certain philosophical insistences of Pierce, such as his veto of an internal improvements bill in the summer of 1854 on the basis of his principles. He did not believe in federal support of state or regional improvements. Thus in the summer of 1854, the Western senators and representatives said bitterly that they had received no consideration whatsoever from the administration. This feeling did not help matters a bit, particularly because it set an atmosphere for a political maneuver that was bubbling that summer. Pierce's position was deteriorating every day. On the last day of the congressional session, he went to the Capitol, accompanied by his cabinet, and signed several appropriations and other bills just passed. He was ready to leave the Capitol at two o'clock and walked into the rotunda with two aides to wait for his carriage. Here he was accosted by a young drunk who shook hands, then insisted that the President have a drink with him. Since liquor was always Pierce's enemy, he refused, rather coldly, and the young man began telling him of all the important people he had drunk with in the past. The carriage arrived, the President turned on his heel and began to get in, and the young man threw a hard-boiled egg at him. Pierce was hit in the back. He turned around and had the young man arrested, but later withdrew the complaint. Still, the assault indicated the standing of Pierce's administration.

10

KANSAS AND NEBRASKA II

The summer of 1854 represented the beginning of the end of all Franklin Pierce's hopes of being a positive President, who could lead the country along the path he had chosen for it. Until the end of the congressional session that summer, by whipping and driving, by shoring up one position after another, he had managed to secure the measures he wanted most: the enlargement of the navy and an increase in army pay. He had vetoed several measures and his vetoes had been sustained; he had maintained an "economy" administration and secured passage of several treaties. He realized that his accomplishments were largely defensive, but he felt that this fact could be attributed to the Kansas-Nebraska struggle, and that when he signed the law, he had, indeed, put an end to the slavery issue.

But even before the end of Congress, senators and representatives had left Washington to show how wrong he was. In the beginning, at a small meeting in February, at Ripon, Wisconsin, Whigs, Democrats, Free-Soilers, and others had talked about establishing a new party to fight the existence of slavery in the territories. In July, Michigan politicians adopted the name *Republican* at a meeting in Jackson and then set forth their ideas. They demanded the repeal of the Kansas-Nebraska Act, the abolition of slavery in the District of Columbia and the repeal of the Fugitive Slave Law. Each and every one of these issues had been faced by Pierce before, and he had put them down; he was determined that they should stay down, for through them would arise a renewal of the sectional conflict he detested. That summer the meetings came fast. Starting in the Middle West, they spread to the East—Wisconsin, Ohio, Indiana, Vermont. Everywhere the cry was the same—"Repeal the Kansas-Nebraska Act. Down with slavery."

Franklin Pierce was not particularly conscious of the intensity of this ground swell that occurred in the summer of 1854. Congress left Washington in the heat of August, and he planned a little rest. With Jane and Jefferson Davis and aides who were personal friends, he went to Capon Springs, Virginia, for a week in order to escape the heat and tedium of the capital. He was not annoyed, he said, with the slender results of the congressional session. He was not worried.

He returned to Washington in September and, for a change, considered the political situation, particularly since it was a congressional election year. He was optimistic, although he was aware of the intentions of independent Democrats and others in the West and Northeast to form a new movement. It was distressing that these groups seemed bent on defeating the Democrats who had voted for the Kansas-Nebraska Bill. But of equal importance, perhaps of even more importance to Pierce this summer, was another political development. Cardinal Bedini, the Papal Nuncio from Rome, had come to the United States early in the year on a tour, and his trip had been a signal for an active revival of the anti-Catholic feeling that had swept the country from time to time. At various places in the country, the American or Know-Nothing party was growing very strong, Pierce thought it was growing much stronger

President Franklin Pierce
photo: The Bettmann Archive

than it should since it was based almost completely on prejudice. The Know-Nothings were violently anti-Catholic and equally violent in their opposition to immigration. Their program called for exclusion of Catholics from public office and exclusion of immigrants of all faiths. Further, they said, an immigrant should have to remain in the United States for 21 years and obey all the laws before he could achieve citizenship.

The Know-Nothings had shown strength in Pierce's New Hampshire and other Eastern states. In the spring local elections not much was proved, but Pierce was learning that by midsummer the anti-Nebraska forces were becoming a serious threat. Things were not helped much by Pierce's insistence that the Fugitive Slave Law be enforced vigorously, and his approval of a U.S. Marshal who had arrested three runaway slaves in the spring. The marshal had to call in troops to take them away from an enraged mob, and he then sent one of the slaves back South in a revenue cutter—a federal ship.

Here is a typical Abolitionist reaction, in a letter Pierce received from Boston. "To the chief slave catcher of the United States: You damned infernal scoundrel, if I only had you here in Boston I would murder you." The President did make one gesture, typical of him, which could well have been the beginning of the end of American efforts to capture foreign trade. In the past few years, as the steamboat became more powerful and steamships were built to cross the Atlantic, there had grown up a vigorous competition among various American firms as well as several British firms. One of the most successful of the American firms was the Collins line, which secured a mail subsidy—a guarantee of funds for maintaining regular steamship crossings. Commodore Vanderbilt and others did not like the subsidies which were going to Collins, and Pierce did not like subsidies either. He felt the government was getting too close to business. So, when the appropriation bill for the Collins line came up in 1855, Pierce vetoed it, and his veto was narrowly upheld. The Collins line failed not long after. But the Vanderbilt line as well as the others were never able to maintain regular service, and the subsidized British lines— particularly the Cunard line—began to steal the shipping business of the Western world. The finishing touches would be put on the American merchant marine by the exigencies of the Civil War, but the beginnings of the decline came with Pierce's veto.

Little that was positive was accomplished at the winter congressional session of 1854–1855. There was little that the administration proposed that demanded congressional intervention. The navy and the army were again strengthened, laws were passed to increase the safety factor in steamer travel, a telegraph line to the Pacific was begun, and homesteads were granted to all veterans; but that was about all. Congress suffered from a lack of leadership. The country was discomfited and sullen, without quite knowing why. Perhaps the events in Kansas were the reason.

In Kansas and Nebraska, trouble had begun almost immediately after the passage of the legislation authorizing the territories. President Pierce had tried to avoid trouble by appointing a Northern man to be governor of Kansas and a Southern man to be governor of Nebraska. To govern Kansas he appointed Andrew H. Reeder of Pennsylvania. Immediately the whole idea and the man were suspect by the South, whose hotheads claimed that the appointment was *prima facie* evidence that Pierce intended to turn Kansas into a free state.

Perhaps a genius could have made sure that Kansas would be properly handled and governed, given all the opposing forces that centered there in 1854. But consider them. First, there were the land speculators, not the last of whom was Governor Reeder himself. As soon as the Kansas territory was opened, the speculators rushed in and began to buy up lands. Reeder was deeply involved in this matter. Second was the

Emigrant Aid Company of New England, which put up money and brought armed settlers in from the North with the avowed purpose of making Kansas into a free territory. Third was the Indian population and the Indian agents, trying to protect their protégés from the ravages of the speculators and settlers. Fourth were the Missourians, led by Senator Atchison and other strong characters, who responded to the Emigrant Aid Company's efforts by encouraging armed Southern slaveowners to come in. Given these factors, and the heady emotion of the times, it is not hard to see that trouble was coming.

Reeder was appointed governor on June 29, 1854, and a man more concerned with purely gubernatorial matters would obviously have gone to the scene, because it was well known that there would be complications in Kansas. But Reeder had affairs of his own to handle and he did not even set out for Kansas until autumn, by which time the complications were well begun. Southerners, infiltrating in from the West, were carrying guns and intimidating those whom they could. Northerners were coming in with New England money to maintain Free-Soil. And above all, there were the frauds in Indian and other lands, which could be easily acquired by soldiers and anyone else under the federal land laws. Some squatters began taking over lands belonging to the Delaware Indians, and troops drove them off. This complication added to the emotionalism of the day. The Indian agents did not feel that Governor Reeder was doing his job, and they complained to President Pierce. Reeder, on his arrival at Fort Leavenworth, spoke out against those in Washington who were "interfering."

By autumn matters were in a pretty mess. The land dealings were confused and improper. Some 2,000 armed men from western Missouri had invaded the area and were terrorizing inhabitants. A territorial delegate to Congress was elected that fall, and the election was a fraud. The Southerners had triumphed by intimidation and John W. Whitfield, the candidate of the Southerners, won. But this caused the New Englanders to pour in more money and bring in more armed men of their own.

Meanwhile, Governor Reeder was in trouble. His dealings involving Indian lands came before Commissioner Manypenny and the latter objected strenuously to the governor's attempt to enrich himself from the public weal. Manypenny denounced Reeder to Pierce, and before long the President had Reeder before him and was trying to work out a compromise that would leave Kansas in peace. Pierce's efforts were well-meaning, but too complex to be successful. What he tried to do was remove an incompetent and voracious official, without indicating that Reeder had done anything wrong. Reeder saw that the President would be embarrassed by his removal, and made things very difficult. For a time, Pierce hoped to remove Reeder while making it appear that he approved of the man's actions by giving him another job (American minister to China, it was said) and send in a new man to clean up the Kansas mess. Obviously, while all this maneuvering was going on in Washington, the governing of Kansas was left in default and, in that sense, Pierce must bear personal responsibility for much of what happened afterward.

The affair broadened on March 30, when local elections were held in Kansas to choose a territorial legislature. The Missourians, angry over the activities of the Emigrant Aid Company, staged a *coup* in the elections, sending in their men who voted fraudulently and intimidated others. The result was a proslavery legislature. It might have been elected anyway, for there were many legitimate Southern settlers in Kansas. But the facts will never be known and are still disputed by historians. Governor Reeder accepted the legislature (some say he was threatened, intimidated and thus forced to do so). He issued a call for a meeting at Pawnee in July. He was still not free from cupidity. For Reeder owned land around Pawnee and was apparently trying to locate the capital in the territory that he owned. This action infuriated many people. Reeder went to the East to seek political support and, while in Pennsylvania, made a speech charging that the Missourians had taken the territory fraudulently.

When Senator Atchison read an account of that speech he was furious and he recounted all of Reeder's sins publicly, demanding that the governor be removed. The problem was thrown at Pierce.

The President wanted Kansas to be free, and he was certain that, under normal circumstances, slavery had no place there. But he wanted to get rid of Reeder, so he put his plan of change into motion. Reeder mishandled himself, his greed was still showing, and the plan came to nothing. Finally, Secretary of State Marcy and Caleb Cushing persuaded Pierce that Reeder must have another chance to make good and straighten out the mess, lest Kansas be victimized. Pierce reluctantly agreed, but when Reeder returned to Kansas and began quarreling with the legislature and important citizens, Pierce removed him, at the end of July. He also removed several others involved in the Pawnee City transactions, and Pawnee City was destroyed and returned to the Indians.

Now the Southerners claimed that because the election had shown that Kansas was partial to the Southern cause, a Southerner must be made governor. Pierce ignored them and chose Wilson Shannon, who had been governor of Ohio, and who was neutral on the question of slaveholding. Pierce hoped for a new start.

11

"TREASON" IN KANSAS

When Congress convened in December, 1855, President Pierce's annual message devoted only a paragraph to Kansas, stating that while there had been troubles there, in his opinion, nothing had occurred to bring about federal intervention. Another President might have felt quite differently, for much had occurred in Kansas since the recall of Governor Reeder.

The proslavery legislature had enacted several statutes favorable to slavery. One of these called for a test oath for office-holders which reflected a favorable attitude toward slavery. In September, the antislavery colonists met alone, repudiated the legislature and asked for the admission of Kansas as a free state. From the Emigrant Aid Company, arms began to pour into Kansas and go into the hands of the Northerners. James H. Lane took command of the "Free State" forces. Late in October, the Free-State men met at Topeka and drew up their own constitution, prohibiting slavery but also keeping Negroes out of the territory. Kansas, at this moment, was on the way to having dual governments and opposing armies, so President Pierce's optimism about that situation was anything but justified. Yet most of his message dealt with other problems. He was preoccupied with foreign affairs, particularly with American relations with Great Britain, which were then very tenuous.

Pierce's message to Congress was prepared well before the day the Congress was to meet, and he was considering political life as it had been in the past. But on December 3, 1855, when Congress actually met, life was nothing like it had been in Washington. For the first time in his memory, the House failed to organize, and the Democratic nominee for speaker had 40 votes less then he needed. An old enemy of Pierce's, John P. Hale, again became senator from New Hampshire. And worst of all—on that very day—the new governor of Kansas, Governor Shannon, called for federal troops to support law and order in Kansas. Everything that Pierce had hoped for was crumbling. The failure of the House to organize destroyed Pierce's position with the British, because they maintained that the United States government was not representative of much of anything at that moment. Finally, Pierce sent his annual message up to Capitol Hill, before the organization of the House, and it was read in the Senate. He sent word to the British that he was demanding the recall of the British ambassador for recruiting British troops on American soil to fight their wars in Europe.

By the end of January, Pierce was conscious of the danger in Kansas (he called it revolution) and he so advised Congress in a much longer message. As Chief Executive, Pierce's inclination was to uphold the "duly constituted" government elected in the summer against the Topeka government elected by the Free-Soilers in the fall. He placed the soldiers at the disposal of the original government, but he did make two definite recommendations to Congress about Kansas. First, he called for a constitutional convention and the speedy admission of Kansas as a state. Second, he called for a special appropriation to cover the costs of sending and maintaining an army of federal troops in Kansas.

Matters were delayed, because the House still could not agree on a speaker. But, in February, the House elected Nathaniel Banks, a Republican. This, of course, complicated Pierce's situation because Kansas would certainly now remain a political issue in Washington as well as in the West. In Kansas, affairs were serious. In January, the Free-Staters had elected their own governor and legislature, and blood was being shed in the Wakarusa War and its aftermath. And Reeder had been elected by the Free-Soilers as the congressional representative of their government, just to complicate matters and to add more fuel to the flames. In a message to Congress on February 11, Pierce made it quite plain that he was committed to support the original, or proslavery government group, although he called down criticism on the excesses of both sides. In February, also, Governor Shannon came to Washington to see Pierce, and went back quickly with federal troops at his disposal. Senator Douglas prepared a statehood bill in the Senate. On March 12 it was ready, authorizing Kansas to form a state government as soon as she had 93,000 people, which would entitle her to one congressman. Just then there were only about 30,000 people in the territory.

Naturally the bill was an invitation to both sides, North and South, to pack Kansas as quickly as possible. The Republicans chose it as their major issue and began stirring up resentment against the South. It was an election year. There could not have been a finer political issue for the day. Had Pierce, in that December and January, declared Kansas to be in a state of chaos and discouraged the idea of quick statehood, things might have been quite different. But as far as history was concerned, he made precisely the wrong move at the wrong time. He gave his political enemies an issue that might have been manufactured for them. And, ironically, the Southerners took the position that Pierce had created the whole problem specifically to make sure that Kansas came in as a free state. He was blamed by the South for appointing Reeder and by the North for removing him. From this point on, Pierce had lost control. He had hopes of succeeding himself as President. But the events of the next few months put the idea squarely out of the mind of the nation. Pierce had the support of only part of the South and of federal officeholders.

Pierce was troubled in a new way that spring by foreign affairs. William Walker, a filibuster, had invaded Nicaragua, supported by Commodore Vanderbilt and the Accessory Transit Company, and after seizing that government, put in a puppet President. The American minister to Nicaragua had indicated recognition, but Pierce withdrew the offer. He would labor with the problem caused by an American seizing a friendly nation and all the British disturbance because of it, but he would not solve it in the few remaining months before the elections. Finally, the irritations became so great that Walker's government was recognized, and when the British refused to withdraw their man Crampton, he was dismissed by Pierce as *persona non grata*.

Yet all this trouble was nothing compared to the difficulties that were springing up in Kansas, and as they arose and men's tempers flared high, it seemed that a new kind of violence assailed the whole nation. Examine this record:

May 8, 1856. Rep. Herbert of California murdered a waiter at the Willard Hotel. John Heiss, a Pierce envoy, beat up the editor of the Washington *Star* over an article on Nicaragua.

May 14. Violence broke out in Kansas.

May 21. Lawrence, Kansas, was sacked and burned with the loss of two lives.

May 22. Preston Brooks, a Southerner, entered the Senate chamber and beat Senator Sumner half to death, causing Northern senators to begin wearing guns.

May 24. John Brown led the Pottawatomie massacre, murdering five proslavery colonists near Dutch Henry's Crossing.

May 25. Kansas became an armed camp.

As the Democratic National Convention was about to begin at Cincinnati, all this news assailed the eyes and ears of the delegates, and in spite of Governor Shannon's warnings, the armed men in Kansas gave no indication of settling down.

As far as politics was concerned, Pierce and Senator Douglas were now tied firmly together by the Kansas-Nebraska Act and all the trouble it had brought. Particularly, the Brooks-Sumner fracas had brought a schism to the Democratic party, and men were gathering in little knots in Cincinnati to discuss what had happened.

Some took Brooks's side. Certainly he had been given provocation, for during the congressional debates over Kansas, Senator Sumner had passed all bounds of decency in the bitterness of his tirades against the slaveholders, and he had personally insulted Andrew P. Butler, the senator from South Carolina, who was Brooks's uncle. However, the beating Brooks had administered to Sumner with his cane had very nearly crippled the older man for life. And, by the time of the convention, it was clear from the actions of the Southerners in Congress that they approved. Brooks was lionized in Southern quarters, but the Northern members were inclined to be very critical of him and his supporters.

Given this situation, the warlike acts in Kansas and the news of the Pottawatomie massacre, Pierce's stock was not running high on the eve of the convention. He did not help much by vetoing two internal improvements bills just then, one in be-

half of the South and one in behalf of Michigan. Still, he hoped
to be nominated by the convention for a second term in office.
The Seventh National Convention of the Democratic party
met on June 2 at Cincinnati under Robert McLane, chairman
of the National Committee. John E. Ward of Georgia was
soon chosen President. The two-thirds rule was adopted again,
although some objected that this was no time for demanding
such a large margin; others said it was a time when near
unanimity was needed. Pierce, who remained in Washington,
whiled away his time by reading the newspapers, visiting the
Smithsonian Institution—and hoping. He, Buchanan and
Douglas were the leading candidates; he and Douglas were
favored by the Southerners, by and large. But the Pierce weakness in the North became apparent immediately, and so did
that of Douglas who was hitched to the same Kansas-Nebraska
vehicle. Luckily for Buchanan, as American minister to England, he had been away almost all of this time, overseeing
American interests in England. If our affairs with England
were not as satisfactory as might be hoped, as has been noted,
the American people really were far more concerned about
internal problems to worry too much about England and what
might have aroused them to white heat a score of years earlier.

At Cincinnati, Senator Slidell and several others, who detested Pierce for one reason or another, began working in favor
of Buchanan. On the eve of the convention, the President's
supporters figured he would have 145 votes at the beginning
and Douglas would have 40 that might be converted to votes
for Pierce. But 198 votes were needed under the two-thirds
rule. And then, just before the convention, it became clear that
nothing could be counted on, and that Pierce's hopes were very
dim because Southerners and Northern Democrats were sure
of one thing—they needed what in the 1970's would be called
a low image if they were to win the election. They needed

someone who could not be identified with the rapidly smoking Kansas-Nebraska struggle.

Monday, Tuesday and Wednesday of the convention went by casually enough. The platform was adopted, accepting the Kansas-Nebraska Act principle, without mentioning Franklin Pierce. What Pierce needed was the admission of the "Soft" delegation, the people who were most inclined to his views—from New York State, where there was a contest between these "Softs" and the "Hards" again. But the Credentials Committee report was not accepted by the whole convention. Instead of the admission of the New York "Softs," which would have given Pierce the nomination, the "Softs" and "Hards" split the seats from New York, which put Pierce in an awkward position.

Thursday brought the first ballot. Pierce was unhappy to learn that on that ballot Buchanan led: 135½ votes to his 122½. Douglas had 33 and Cass had five. Pierce did not even have his 145 votes on that first ballot. Parts of the Kentucky, Massachusetts and Ohio delegations had let him down. And in 1852, Pierce had been nominated by the Virginians, who this year dropped him completely in favor of Buchanan.

The handwriting was on the wall, and in Washington Pierce's spirits dropped. So did his support, after the first five ballots. On the sixth ballot he lost Tennessee, and on the seventh he lost Arkansas, Georgia and Kentucky. But it was a contest. Fourteen ballots were held that day, going into the night. The convention adjourned, the delegates moved from one smoke-filled room to another making "deals" and the Pierce men dropped the President that night in an effort to try to nominate Douglas instead and preserve the principles involved. The next morning, Pierce's name was withdrawn in favor of Douglas's, and it then became apparent that there was an effort to stop Buchanan and force a compromise candidate.

But Douglas reached 122 votes, and was stopped. For Douglas it was all right. Buchanan was not expected to seek a second term, and he was looking forward to 1860. For Pierce it was a tragedy. He faced the same problem at the 1856 convention that had brought about his nomination four years earlier. The party was suffering from too many splitting influences and needed a man who was not controversial, particularly on the issue of slavery in the territories. Pierce had come to office sure that the Compromise of 1850 had solved the problem. He had discovered that the Kansas-Nebraska Bill and the issue of "bleeding Kansas" had changed everything, or changed nothing. The juggernaut was moving. There was no hope that anything Pierce might do as late as 1855 could change things for him really, but he never knew it. The conservatives of the party wanted a safe man who could take Whig votes and Know-Nothing votes without inflaming the people on the issue of slavery. Buchanan's absence from the United States during these important years worked for the Pennsylvanian.

Oh, the delegates were generous to Pierce in these last bitter moments. Once Buchanan was nominated, they spoke highly of their President. They passed a resolution praising him and the administration they were not willing to return to office. They said,

> . . . the administration of Franklin Pierce has been true to the great interests of the country. In the face of the most determined opposition, it has maintained the laws, enforced economy, fostered progress and infused integrity and vigor into every department of the government at home. It has signally improved our treaty relations, extending the field of commercial enterprise and vindicated the rights of American citizens abroad. It has asserted with eminent impartiality the just claims of every

section and has at all times been faithful to the Constitution.

The convention approved wholeheartedly of everything Pierce had done, but being pragmatic politicians, the delegates knew that Pierce could not win for them again in the shadow of Kansas and Nebraska. So they dumped the President of the United States.

12

DISAPPOINTMENT

Franklin Pierce was a brave man. On Saturday night after the nomination and the bitter pill of defeat was swallowed, 5,000 people of Washington came to the White House lawn and the President went to an upper window and spoke to them. Mustering his resources, he smiled and said that he completely endorsed the nomination of James Buchanan to the presidency of the United States. It was principles that were important, not people. And he would stand on principle.

Pierce hoped to make one last contribution to America in his days as "lame duck" President: He wanted to solve the Kansas problem once and for all and he turned his mind to this matter. From Kansas came pleas for federal troops and arguments for their use to preserve order in the shattered peace of the territory. Pierce sent a batch of telegrams that summer, the import of them being to persuade the authorities in Kansas to use the federal troops sparingly, to preserve order and enforce the law and to go no further.

But it was impossible to separate politics from Kansas. The Whigs and their friends wanted to send General Winfield

Scott to Kansas to quell the uprising. Pierce recognized the danger, but being a political creature himself, he sent General Persifor F. Smith, a good Democrat.

In Philadelphia, the Republicans met and established a truly national organization. They nominated John C. Frémont for the presidency and put together a platform that depended very heavily on raising sympathy for "bleeding Kansas" and the Free-Soil position that Kansas *must* come in as a free state. Politics again.

Pierce had great hopes for one measure that might resolve the problems of Kansas; it was called the Toombs Bill. This act provided for a census to be taken in Kansas and then for an election to be held. Only those who had lived there for three months or more, at the time of the census, could vote. Thus neither the North nor the South could send in an army of squatters. The vote would elect members of a constitutional convention, who would prepare a constitution and solve the problem of slavery or freedom for the state. To Pierce's mind, this would preserve the forms and the principle of constitutionalism that he had argued for so long. Northern Democrats liked it for the same reason. Southern Democrats liked it because they were losing Kansas to Northern forces and the guns of the Emigrant Aid Company. The Southerners who toured Kansas at about this time said there was about a 50-50 chance that Kansas would go slave if left alone. The Senate passed the bill. But the House, dominated by Whigs and Know-Nothings, sneered at the President and continued to ferment trouble over Kansas. The House did not even really consider the bill. There was politics with a vengeance.

Kansas was split by civil war. Governor Shannon soon proved to be unable to preserve order. Several cases of treason were brought to the federal courts. The troubles continued. At the end of July, Pierce removed Shannon and appointed John W. Geary of Pennsylvania as governor.

A new difficulty was posed by the anti-Democratic House of Representatives. Since the organized forces of the North were winning the Kansas civil war, the House majority was very much opposed to the use of troops and the restoration of order. That, of course, was not the way the Republicans and Know-Nothings put it, but that was the result of their behavior. So the House put a rider on the army appropriation bill which forbade the President to use federal troops to enforce the laws of any territorial legislature. Quite probably the rider was unconstitutional, but there was no time to put it to a test. The Senate refused to accept the rider, and the result was that the army did not get paid. Congress attempted to adjourn, leaving this mess, but Pierce would not let them. He had a powerful weapon against their restlessness and eagerness to go home and play politics before the election of 1856. He immediately called a special session.

Meanwhile the armories were closed and the workers were laid off. There was no money to move troops. Knowing this, James Lane invaded Kansas with an army of Free-Soilers, and the Missourians threatened to come in with great force and cut Lane down. Only because of this general fear, with armies of both sides waiting, did the politicians of the House finally relent. They passed an army pay bill without restrictions on the President's power to use the army to preserve order.

Once Congress adjourned, and the legislators left Washington, Pierce attempted to preserve order in Kansas by issuing specific instructions to the troops. Secretary of War Davis ordered the governors of Illinois and Kentucky to have militia ready to go in and preserve order, if necessary. There was to be no rebellion in Kansas. Peace was to be restored and the law obeyed. General Smith was to be the instrument of the federal authorities, and he managed to the extent that no open rebellion succeeded, although the territory was filled with rebellions and heavily armed men. On September 27, Pierce heard from

General Smith that he had peacefully turned back an army of 1,000 armed Missourians who were bent on marching into Kansas and fighting the Free-Soilers.

That fall, President Pierce took a trip back to Concord to make ready for his homecoming. He was well received by the people at large but not by old political friends and he noticed the cut very quickly.

The visit over, he went back to Washington to await developments and was cheered by the election of Buchanan to the presidency, and the renewed control of Congress by the Democrats. Looking back, he felt that Buchanan ought to have an easier time of it, since so much of his own troubles had come about after the 1856 election of the anti-Democratic majority had blocked his efforts to make Congress do the administration's bidding in the matter of Kansas.

Granted a measure of peace by the knowlege that "principle" still had triumphed, Pierce set about disengaging himself from Washington and accounting for his stewardship of the administrative facilities of the nation. They were peculiar to their time. The government had disposed of nearly 94,000,000 acres of land, which meant profits for the people who got the land as well as westward expansion and consolidation of the American continent. Pensions and patents were in fairly good shape; more Indian treaties (52 of them) had been signed for later administrations to break. The national debt had been reduced to $31,000,000, but the federal surplus continued and Congress refused to reduce the tariff three times. The army was in good shape and had done a good job of keeping down Indian insurrections in the Far West and controlling affairs in Kansas as much as the politicians would allow. The six new frigates that represented the navy expansion were in the process of being built.

The Perry mission to Japan had brought its own successes and Townsend Harris, a New York businessman, had gone to

Japan to follow up on the treaty that opened the country to commerce. Temporarily, at least, the difficulties with Great Britain were settled. William Walker continued to be in power in Nicaragua, but that matter was beyond Pierce's power to resolve at the time. The problem of the Mosquito Indians on the east coast of Central America might be solved; Britain and America were talking about a treaty to guarantee their safety, and certain rights of Costa Rica on the San Juan River, with Greytown—the source of so much trouble—becoming a free port. There were other details; Britain was indicating a willingness to settle many old arguments in Latin America.

Late in November, Pierce worked on his final State of the Union Address and fell ill in doing so, probably from his old malaria which he had contracted during the Mexican campaign. There was more trouble with Kansas, emanating from charges that Chief Justice Lecompte of the territorial courts was behaving improperly. This became a problem toward the end of the year—one that was not resolved because of bureaucratic difficulties in the appointments of new judges for the territory. And yet, Pierce ended the year with the hope that peace had been brought to Kansas and the problem of its admission to the Union finally settled. In fact, matters did quiet down there, giving him reason for his hopes, and he was not to know that the Kansans were only waiting for a new administration and new action.

The early months of 1857 moved by swiftly and, on February 24, Pierce held the last Tuesday afternoon reception that he would ever give and prepared for one final party on Friday evening. Most of Washington came, and the party was a huge success, for if Pierce had not been popular in the North—and had been the victim of partisan politics—he was personally an attractive man. Washington, which could share his views of the Kansas situation, could sympathize with a problem that looked far more simple elsewhere.

There were a few more presidential problems; new treaties brought up from Mexico, filibustering problems in Latin America, new ideas for better relations with Britain and with France, and Kansas would not stay quiet, even at the last. Judge Lecompte, whose removal Pierce had instigated, struggled against it, and using Southern influence, managed to keep his position in Kansas, much to the resentment of the Free-Soil men. His name would go down in history, because a town was called after him (Lecompton) and the legislature met there and devised the famous Lecompton Constitution which exacerbated the Kansas question in the next two years.

Finally on March 3, 1857, it was all over for Franklin Pierce as President of the United States. Jane Pierce said farewell to the White House without the slightest regret—she had hated these four years. She left and went to stay with Secretary Marcy and his wife in Washington, for the weather in New Hampshire was considered to be still too harsh for her health. Next day, after turning over the government to James Buchanan, Pierce joined Jane at the Marcys. His last hours as President brought nothing particularly pleasing or alarming, except the one spot of pleasure at signing, just before he quit, a bill that reduced the tariff—something which he had been trying to do for four years.

So President Pierce retired. He had no financial worries, because he had been able to save half his presidential salary of $25,000 each year. At the end of his term he had $78,000 invested, which would keep him very comfortably for the rest of his life. Since all his children were dead, he had no one to look after except himself and Jane. His responsibility to Jane weighed heavily on Pierce because he had neglected her in favor of the public business for four years. Now, to make up for lost time, he took her abroad, and dedicated much of his time to trying to relieve the melancholy mood that had become a part of her. She was dreadfully depressed and never seemed to be able to change.

The Pierces stayed with the Marcys until late spring and then went to Massachusetts and New Hampshire. At Massachusetts' Fanueil Hall, Pierce spoke stridently of the need for Americans to behave as Americans and not as Northerners and Southerners, slaveowners and Abolitionists, if the good that had come of the federal Union was to be preserved. There was no mistaking his sincerity or his forcefulness. Yet in the North, fewer and fewer people were listening.

The Pierces remained in New England during the summer, and, in the fall, they decided to go abroad. When President Buchanan learned of their trip, he offered them the use of the government ship *Powhatan* for passage. They went first to Madeira, the Portuguese island in the Atlantic Ocean, and then to tour Western Europe. They visited Portugal, Spain, France, Switzerland, Italy, Austria, Germany, Belgium and England that year. They spent the summer of 1858 at Lake Geneva and the winter in Italy. Pierce looked up old friends who were abroad, especially Nathaniel Hawthorne, with whom he had a joyful reunion in Rome. But Hawthorne noted Pierce's white hair, his lined face, and said later that he felt that the presidency had used Pierce hard, that the four years had sapped something from him, some quality that could never be regained.

Poor America! In a way, Pierce was pleased to read that Buchanan was faring no better than he had himself, but in another way it was saddening to sit abroad and watch from the distance as his native country tore itself apart. The longing became too great, and in the summer of 1859, the Pierces returned to Boston. It was nearly three years since Pierce had left the presidency.

Once again, the Democrats were searching for someone who might unite the country, so badly split now, so much more at

odds than it was in 1857 when Pierce had gone away. The Dred
Scott decision had come, which infuriated the Northern Abolitionists and those who feared the spread of slavery, because it
held that Negro slaves were not citizens, that temporary residence by a slave in a free state did not free him, and that the
Missouri Compromise, which had outlawed slavery in 1820 in
the territories, was unconstitutional. Of course, Pierce had
always said the Missouri Compromise was unconstitutional and
that the Compromise of 1850 effectively settled the issue without raking open old wounds. That's why many Southerners
were talking about Pierce.

Another issue had developed in Kansas, or one might say the
Kansas troubles had followed the course that might have been
expected, given two groups of armed men, one group determined to uphold slavery in the territory by force and the other
group determined to put it down. The constitution drawn at
Lecompton, which guaranteed the right of men to keep slaves
in Kansas, was drastically voted down by the people when it
came before them. President Buchanan said the plebescite was
illegal, and submitted the constitution to Congress, which
brought about an open breach between free and slave contin-
gents in the Congress. The Lecompton Constitution was again
submitted to the Kansans under federal auspices, and Kansans
voted to remain territorial citizens rather than have so divided
a state.

Thus was violence ended in Kansas, and peace brought to
that troubled area for the first time in years. But the issue
remained to upset Democrats and give Republicans something
to shout about. Republican Abraham Lincoln and Democrat
Stephen A. Douglas debated the questions of slavery and Kansas in a series of meetings in 1858, and it became apparent to
all that eventually America would have to become either tolerant of slavery everywhere in the Union, or reject slavery altogether. William H. Seward of New York, the leading Repub-

lican figure in the Senate, said as much in the fall of 1858, more or less putting a cap on the subject of the Lincoln-Doulgas debates.

In the fall of 1859 came John Brown's raid on Harpers Ferry, and his capture, trial and execution. Pierce took the position that Brown was a fanatic, trying to use Kansas tactics for the destruction of the whole country. Pierce continued to hold that slavery was constitutional and the North would have to learn to live with it.

This position made Pierce very much a favorite of the Southerners, and a number of them suggested to him privately in Boston that he might run again for the presidency in 1860. Pierce declined to have his name submitted or to consider it, and he meant it. He had no further desire to be a politician except in local New Hampshire affairs. He bought 60 acres on Pleasant Street in Concord, a long thoroughfare that runs west out of the heart of the city. When winter came, he decided for Jane's sake that they would visit the West Indies, and thus avoid the cold weather again. While waiting to leave for Nassau, Pierce dabbled a little in national politics because no former President can remain free of such interest. People asked and he said that he thought the best Democratic candidate in 1860 would be Jefferson Davis, who had been completely loyal to him as Secretary of War in the cabinet of the early 1850's.

After a winter spent pleasantly idling in the West Indies, Pierce and Jane came home in June to discover that the nation was in a turmoil and the Democratic party for which Pierce had struggled so many years had split squarely in two. Caleb Cushing and other old friends tried to convince Pierce that he, and he alone, could bring the warring factions together. Pierce said no, that he could not and he would not even attempt it for he was no "leader of forlorn hopes." Even had he been so inclined, he told friends, that he would still have refused, because his beloved Jane was very, very ill and even the idea

The residence of General Pierce, Concord, New Hampshire
photo: *The Bettmann Archive*

of having to return to Washington would be destructive to her.
No, Pierce was finished with participation in national politics. His only concern now was with the preservation of the
nation.

13

THE END
OF HOPE

Before the election of 1860, the Democrats knew that their internal division would bring them down to defeat. On the one hand was Stephen A. Douglas, the candidate of the moderates and Free-Soil men who had remained in the Democratic party. On the other hand was John Breckinridge, the candidate of the South. Several people talked to Pierce about becoming a compromise candidate even then; they argued that if he would let his name be used, perhaps Breckinridge and Douglas could be persuaded to withdraw in his favor. Probably it was a wild dream, but it would never be tested because Pierce refused. The idea appealed to him—the idea of a compromise candidate—and he suggested James Guthrie, his former Secretary of the Treasury. Jefferson Davis and others suggested this course to several leaders, but nothing came of it.

Once the election was lost, and the South began to act to withdraw from the Union, state by state, friends pleaded with Pierce to step in and try to persuade them not to leave. But Pierce really sympathized with the South. He was so welded to his belief that slavery was guaranteed under the states' rights provisions of the Constitution, and could not be interfered with legally, that he failed to realize that there was a higher law than the Constitution of any country—the law of humanity. He spoke out, but against coercion by the North. He did not realize that the Northern people were increasingly behind the Abolitionists at this time, and that Abolition would be the key to the union of the North against the South, and that it must grow rather than diminish.

In Washington, the federal government was planning to send commissioners to each of the states that were holding conventions that would take them out of the Union. Friends wanted Pierce to become a commissioner to Alabama, but he had no faith in it and had a convenient illness which he could use as a plea. He wrote letters instead, calling on his Southern friends to stay in the Union but the letters had no more effect than his pleas with the Northerners to be gentle with the South.

Former President Tyler went to Washington and tried desperately to find a way out, but not Pierce. He was more pragmatic; he saw no way out, given the points of view expressed both by the North and the South. He believed the North was wrong, and there was no way to appeal to the South unless the North backed away from its incorrect position.

Events marched on. President Buchanan dispatched the ship *Star of the West* to Fort Sumter to provide the fort when it was cut off from supplies by the Southerners. Pierce said the action almost certainly meant war. Then came March 4, and Lincoln's access to the presidency. Then came April 12, when the shore batteries of Charleston opened on the little island in the harbor. Pierce's reaction was to declare his loyalty to the Union, but at the same time he wrote Martin Van Buren, former President, suggesting that the ex-Presidents meet at Philadelphia and make some call for unity. The display would have been impressive: John Tyler would come from Virginia,

Millard Fillmore and Martin Van Buren from New York, Pierce from New Hampshire and James Buchanan from Pennsylvania. But Van Buren, the ranking former President, refused to take any responsibility and suggested that Pierce do it himself. Nothing came of the gesture.

Pierce opposed the war, and he said so. As a result of his open action, he received a letter from Secretary of State Seward nearly accusing Pierce of treason. The Secretary suggested that he was aiding a committee organized to overthrow the government of the United States. The accusation embittered Pierce, as well it might embitter a man who had served as President of the United States and struggled for four years to maintain union where there was very little. As the war went on, he became more bitter. The charges that he was disloyal persisted, and the vicious circle grew tighter. When the administration issued its Emancipation Proclamation, he declared that the Abolitionists had triumphed and the Constitution had been overthrown. And finally on Bunker Hill Day, 1863, Pierce made a strong speech against the war, which alienated so many of his friends that his position was never again the same in the nation or in New Hampshire. To add to his personal troubles, Jane Pierce died on December 2, 1863, and left him quite alone. Hawthorne came to the funeral, but he did not live long either. Hawthorne died in the spring of 1864 and, although they were the dearest of friends, so poor was Pierce's reputation that he could not be included as a pallbearer.

In the political campaign of 1864, the Republicans attempted to destroy Pierce and with him the Democratic party. Letters from Pierce to Jefferson Davis in times past were unearthed, and Pierce's conduct in the Kansas situation was declared to be an attempt to make Kansas a slave state. Since Davis was now President of the Confederacy, these charges stuck, particularly with people too young to know what Pierce had stood for and tried to accomplish. After all, many soldiers and many voters had been merely children in the years 1853–1857 when Pierce had held office, and they were subject to the war propaganda and all the high emotions of the day. Pierce sat in his house in Concord and confined himself to urging a few that they unite on General McClellan as a candidate, which the party did—but to no avail.

Pierce's position was truly shown in the excitement that followed the assassination of Lincoln. Emotions ran high in Concord when the news came, and a mass meeting of loyalty was called in the center of the town. Some mischief-maker shouted that they should go get Pierce, and the crowd moved purposefully toward the house of the former President of the United States.

Pierce was resting when they came. He had a few moments warning from a servant. What did they want? They demanded that every household show a flag.

The crowd arrived jostling and shouting, and Pierce, a small flag in hand, came to the door.

"Where is your flag?" came the rude shout.

Pierce, the former President of the United States, stood up straight before the mob.

"It is not necessary for me to show my devotion for the Stars and Stripes by any special exhibitions . . ." he said. "If the period which I have served our state and country in various situations, commencing more than thirty-five years ago, has left in doubt the question of my devotion to the flag, the Constitution and the Union, it is too late now to rescue it by any such exhibition. . . ."

The old President finished his speech angrily, and the crowd left.

These last years were unhappy ones for the man who had once occupied the seat of power. He drank too much. He spent a great deal of time alone. He changed churches, from Congregational to Episcopal, because he objected to the fulminations of the Rev. Henry Parker in the pulpit of the South Congregational Church. Parker was a stern Abolitionist and believer in punishment for the South. Pierce wanted solace, not diatribe, from his religion and was baptized as an Episcopalian in 1865. Late in life, he bought acreage at Little Boar's Head on the New Hampshire seacoast. He built a cottage there and laid out a subdivision to try to create a summer colony. He was occupying himself as much as anything else, for his fortune was about $90,000, which was ample for his needs. It was a lonely life, knowing that he was detested for holding unpopular views, and that he was thought of by the young as a man who was disloyal to the country, when in fact he had given his own youth and strength to the United States.

In the fall of 1869, when Pierce was 64 years old, he returned to Concord to stay at the home of Willard Williams on South Main Street, and here he fell ill. He was unconscious for three days and sick for a month. He died early on a Friday morning. President Grant proclaimed national mourning and ordered government buildings draped in black. The body was taken for a brief stay in the Concord State House. Mayor Lyman D. Stevens asked merchants to close their stores for an hour at noon on Monday, the day of the funeral, and the schools were dismissed so the children could see the procession. The governor and the mayor were among the pallbearers. Then there was the funeral ceremony at St. Paul's Episcopal Church, followed by a burial in Concord's Old North Cemetery. Finally, there was good said about the sad, old statesman. "Those who knew General Pierce well, loved him well," said the Providence *Journal* on the occasion of his death. "His sweetness of disposition, his unfailing courtesy and gentleness, and his winning manner, attracted many hearts to him. His ear was never closed to any tale of suffering, and his hand was ever stretched out to help the sick and needy."

But in his own New Hampshire, Pierce was scarcely honored for many years. The state legislature finally voted for a memorial to the former President, after many a legislature had ignored the project. All those years New Hampshiremen had voted against Pierce, time and again, because he stood for states' rights on the eve of the Civil War. But then former United States Senator William E. Chandler began the campaign for support, and eventually he persuaded New Hampshireman that they owed a debt of gratitude to the President who had stood for preservation of the Union, which was Pierce's basic position. In 1895, the project was organized. Yet feelings still ran so high that it was 1913 before the legislature voted the funds, and 1914 before the memorial statue was erected in front of the federal post office, near the State House. Poor unhappy man! Fillmore before him and Buchanan after him faced many of the same problems. Of course, the one overriding problem of the era was the issue of slavery in its many manifestations and the growing demand from the North that the "institution" be outlawed in the United States of America.

Throughout history, Pierce is known as one of the weaker of the American Presidents, and his administration is often characterized as "vacillating. And yet, perhaps the most interesting point about the four years of the Pierce administration is the development of the slavery issue from a nagging pain to an overriding problem. It is doubtful if any political leader of the day would have fared much better than Pierce in trying to control Kansas or the slave issue, because the two sides, the North and the South, were engaged in what was aptly defined later as "the irrepressible conflict" over slavery. Pierce did well in his management of foreign affairs, gaining satisfactory treaties with England and other countries. He stood strongly against internal improvements, a very old-fashioned stand, but this was in line with his feeling that every state should take responsibility for its own territory. He believed that if two states shared a river, then they should manage its navigability and other characteristics. There may be a quarrel with the position, but it was, nevertheless, an old Jacksonian idea, and one not uncommon in Pierce's day. Pierce failed in many ways, and yet it is hard to believe that he could have succeeded, given the march of events in America during the years 1853 to 1857. His failure was also the failure of the social system. He, a New Hampshireman, who never had any use for slaves or slavery, paid a bitter price for those early merchants and traders who made fortunes by bringing Negro slaves to North America.

Suggested Readings

Anderson, Leon W., Unpublished research material. Concord, N.H., Office of Legislative Services.

DEDICATION OF A STATUE OF PRESIDENT FRANKLIN PIERCE. Concord, N.H., Rumford Press, 1914.

Hawthorne, Nathaniel, FRANKLIN PIERCE. Boston, 1852.

Hoyt, Edwin P., JAMES BUCHANAN. Chicago, Reilly and Lee, 1966.

——————, MARTIN VAN BUREN. Chicago, Reilly and Lee, 1964.

——————, ZACHARY TAYLOR. Chicago, Reilly and Lee, 1966.

Minor, Henry, THE STORY OF THE DEMOCRATIC PARTY. New York, The Macmillan Co., 1928.

Morison, Samuel E., OXFORD HISTORY OF THE AMERICAN PEOPLE. New York, Oxford University Press, 1965.

Nichols, Roy Franklin, FRANKLIN PIERCE. Philadelphia, University of Pennsylvania Press, 1931.

INDEX

EDWIN P. HOYT's experience as a foreign correspondent has provided the nucleus for many of the books he has written for adults and young readers, as well as numerous articles for newspapers and magazines. When he is not at the typewriter, Mr. Hoyt enjoys traveling and fishing. He and his wife have a permanent home in Vermont.

Other titles by Edwin Hoyt include: JOHN TYLER: the Tenth President of the United States. "Both sources and approach are sound . . . constructive as well as instructive."
The Kirkus Service

THE TRAGIC COMMODORE: The Story of Oliver Hazard Perry. "A good, straight-forward account of a man and a neglected period in United States History."
Library Journal

LELAND STANFORD "The author captures both the man and the period in which he lived. Young readers will appreciate insights into history through the biography of one of the builders of California."
Best Sellers